Easy Scrapbooking

QUARRY

Emma's first experience
well! She really liked cere
was willing to accept the
Until she got her first t

e

firsts. The first
heard your
The first time we
wriggling around
asound. The first
e held you.

is

Easy Scrapbooking

**Use your home computer to create stylish layouts
for weddings, holidays, and other occasions**

patty hoffman brahe of mountaincow

introduction by leslie ayers, *Scrapbook Answers* magazine

GLOUCESTER MASSACHUSETTS

QUARRY BOOKS

First published in the United States of America by
Quarry Books, a member of
Quayside Publishing Group
33 Commercial Street
Gloucester, Massachusetts 01930-5089
Telephone: (978) 282-9590
Fax: (978) 283-2742
www.rockpub.com

Library of Congress Cataloging-in-Publication Data
Brahe, Patty Hoffman.
    Easy scrapbooking: Use your home computer to create stylish layouts for weddings,
  holidays, and other occasions / Patty Hoffman Brahe.
        p. cm.
    ISBN 1-59253-270-5 (pbk.)
    1. Photograph albums—Data processing. 2. Photography—Digital techniques. 3.
Scrapbooks—Data processing. 4. Digital preservation. I. Title.
  TR501.B73 2006
  745.593—dc22   2006012138
                                                                         CIP

ISBN-13: 978-1-59253-270-4
ISBN-10: 1-59253-270-5

10 9 8 7 6 5 4 3 2 1

Layout: Collaborated, Inc.
Wedding Photos in project on page 73 by Brett Matthews; Bat Mitzvah photos in project
on page 105 by Jan Press. Scrapbook project photos by Allan Penn.

Printed in Singapore

Scrapbook Design

Renée Foss and Traci Turchin, both inducted to the 2005 Creating Keepsakes Hall of Fame, are published in *Scrapbooks Etc*, *Simple Scrapbooks*, and *Memory Makers* magazines. Renée is co-owner of Pink Martini Designs, a company that provides teaching kits to scrapbook retailers for in-store classes. Traci serves on the design teams for A Muse Artstamps and Scrapworks as well as contributing articles to leading scrapbook magazines. Ursula Page's layouts have appeared in *PaperKuts*, *Creating Keepsakes*, and *Scrapbooks Etc*. Lara Scott has been published in *2005 CK Idea Book* and *Memory Makers 2005 Rubber Stamper's File*.

Introduction and How-to Videos

Leslie Ayers is editor-in-chief of *Scrapbook Answers* magazine. With twelve years in the publishing business and a lifelong interest in paper crafts, Leslie helped launch the magazine in 2005, which offers readers unparalleled, hands-on instruction and coverage of the hottest scrapbooking techniques, products, and trends.

Acknowledgments

The author greatly appreciates the many contributions from scrapbook designers, retailers, authors, and everyday scrapbookers, without whom this book would not be nearly so helpful and enjoyable. Thank you all so much for sharing your expertise, your photos, and your scrap-worthy moments:

Dawn Ashby, Glynis Astie, Suzanne Barlyn, Chris Brahe, Marika Brahe, Christina Capozzi, Anne Chertoff, Jessica Clark, Sharon Cohen, Erin Connor, Ken Cornick, Lisa Corso, Andrea Crane, Rebecca Dohndt, Jen Drechsler, Jackson Eisen, Judith Eisen, Sabrina Eisen, Rebecca Feld, Dayspring Fowler, Evan Frankel, Kim Hammer, Barney and Diane Hoffman, Eva Hoffman, Sam Hoffman, Jennifer Jones, Skyler Jones, Marisa Karplus, Nick Kelsh, Benjamin Knopf, Lewis Knopf, Pnina Knopf, Wendy Lundgren, Kelly Lynch, Colleen Mahoney, Lisa Martin, Krista Mettler, Amy Morick, Lisa Neighbors, Kathy O'Brien, Heidi Peterson, Alison Rosenthal, Sandy, Rachel Schleich, Linda C. Senn, Justine Shembri, Natalie Williams, Billie Sue Woolley, and Mary Ellen Young.

In addition, the author would like to send thanks to everyone at Quarry Books who have been so helpful during this process, including Winnie Prentiss, Mary Ann Hall, Betsy Gammons, and David Martinell. Finally, special thanks to the team at Mountaincow for their contributions with copyediting, graphic production, and software expertise, including Erin Connors, Megan Eisen, and Josh Eisen.

contents

introduction

SCRAPBOOKING IS MANY THINGS—STORYTELLING, MEMORY KEEPING, photo preservation, visual art, papercrafting, graphic design. There's nothing like creating a scrapbook page, or an entire album, using a variety of traditional supplies: paper, of course, but also paint, ink, chalk, ribbon, embossing materials, and any number of the gorgeous ready-made embellishments available today. But there is tremendous appeal to being able to create pages with a computer that are just as beautiful and have the appearance of being just as three-dimensional. *Easy Scrapbooking*, combined with tools like Mountaincow's scrapbooking software, makes it possible for busy scrapbookers to quickly and easily create all-digital pages or digitally assisted pages that simply wouldn't be possible without technology.

The benefit of using Mountaincow's scrapbooking software is you never have to decide which team you're on; you can dabble in both digital and traditional scrapbooking and get the best of both worlds.

—*Easy Scrapbooking*, Chapter 6

When I read this sentence, I thought, exactly! That's it! That's what we at *Scrapbook Answers* aim to help our readers with in every issue! Longtime scrapbookers sometimes debate the merits of traditional vs. digital scrapbooking. Frankly, this baffles me because I don't see anything wrong with embracing both. To be sure, what drew me to scrapbooking in the first place was the hands-on nature of the craft: cutting, gluing, folding, arranging, tearing, painting, embossing, stamping—just generally, creating. But since we launched *Scrapbook Answers* in the fall of 2005, many talented digital scrapbookers have opened my eyes to the amazing range of possibilities available when using a computer. And it turns out that over ninety-three percent of experienced scrapbookers surveyed said they already use a computer to assist with their scrapbooking! There are so many ways that digital tools such as scanners, photo printers, digital cameras, and software can help us work faster and allow us to create scrapbooks that are even more meaningful—and certainly better examples of good design than they would be otherwise.

No matter how you go about it, scrapbooking is a creative endeavor. It carries personal significance not just for you, the scrapbooker, but for all your family and loved ones—and the generations that follow. You'll know when you get it right—you'll feel happy with the pages you've created, and you'll no doubt receive wonderful feedback from your loved ones when you share the pages with them. Beyond that, technology helps make it easier to do some things just a little faster, to perfect imperfect photos that might otherwise never see the light of day, design your own custom page elements, and create journaling blocks worthy of graphic design awards.

This book is full of fabulous tips and techniques that all scrapbookers can use. In addition to the projects in every single chapter, you'll find an overview of important design principles and color theory, journaling suggestions, photography tips, and tons of page ideas. Get ready to learn a lot—even if you've been scrapbooking for a long time. And for those of you who are really obsessed with the craft, you can learn about Mountaincow's professional scrapbooking software, which could help you turn your obsession into a full-time career. You really don't have to choose between traditional and digital scrapbooking...but you definitely should take a closer look at this book, because you're not going to be able to resist putting the ideas and techniques presented here into practice on your own pages. So read on—and go create!

Leslie Ayers
Editor-in-Chief
Scrapbook Answers magazine
www.scrapbookanswers.com

S

is for summer

smile

Summer is a charming lass, slipping barefoot through the grass.
Rosy-cheeked windswept hair, spreading sunshine everywhere.
Up and down the fields and hills, magic colors Summer spills.
Flowers bloom so bright and gay, Beauty blesses Summer's way.
Beverly Andersson

HARRY

. Dirty or clean. Dressed up or naked as a
d. Cooperative or contrary. Asserting his
ence or still wanting to be the baby. He's
boy, my Harry-Bird, my sweet potato and
me I look at him he just tugs at my heart.
ver he does, he does it in a cute way. Even
pitching a fit he will do something cute.
ll wrapped around his little finger. And
it's no wonder...

He's just too cute.

Y

is for Youth

All Wrapped Up

chapter 1

for everyday moments

Documenting life's milestones is important, but capturing the day-to-day events of your life can be just as meaningful. The commute to work, Sunday morning breakfasts in bed, and nighttime rituals to put your kids to sleep are often the most special of memories. Keep a small digital camera handy at all times to capture these spontaneous moments, and think about composition, background, and contrast when taking the photos. You should then write about the reasons they mean so much in your scrapbooks. Take advantage of the collection of fonts on your computer to create journals in styles that look like handwriting, swirly script, or an old-fashioned typewriter. The fonts will help you communicate the emotions of fleeting memories of everyday things such as a favorite blanket, a faithful pet, or a trip to the grocery store.

 # kids

Capturing everyday moments begins with everyday photos. Suzanne Barlyn, a freelance writer in New Jersey, knows her way around a professional camera. Her family owns a photo studio, so taking pictures is second nature to her. Her professional-grade camera produces fantastic photos but is too cumbersome to throw in a purse or pocket. Not wanting to sacrifice quality, Suzanne carefully researched her digital options and found one small enough for her to bring everywhere.

This means, of course, even a coffee run can turn into a photo shoot. On a recent visit to Dunkin Donuts, Suzanne took photos of her three kids eating donuts, a top shot of the box full of donuts, and some close-ups. She even saved a piece of the box for a layout to add to a special "day to day" album she's starting.

"I have rolls and rolls of my kids at the pool in the summer time, jumping in leaf piles, on their bikes with neighborhood friends, and of my husband putting them to bed," she said. "You're going to forget these little things. You have to take a few moments to take your camera out to get more day-to-day memories."

CAMERA SHY NO MORE

Scrapbook designer Renée Foss says, "At this point, my kids are so used to the camera they don't even stop to smile. They just keep on doing what they're doing—which is great!"

The everyday event pages are the ones Renée likes to scrap best. "You will always photograph things like the first day of school, but besides being a little taller and having a new backpack, the photos are pretty similar from year to year," she says. "You have to get the transient things like the toys they play with or the food they love."

"Sometimes I have something very specific about my children I know I am going to want to remember, like Harry all wrapped up after a bath."

WHAT'S YOUR TYPE?

Once Renée has her photos gathered together and is starting the layout process, she considers her fonts. Her two most important criteria in a font are that they don't upstage the photos and that they are legible.

HARRY

Wet or dry. Dirty or clean. Dressed up or naked as a jaybird. Cooperative or contrary. Asserting his independence or still wanting to be the baby. He's my baby boy, my Harry-Bird, my sweet potato and every time I look at him he just tugs at my heart. Whatever he does, he does it in a cute way. Even when he is pitching a fit he will do something cute. He has us all wrapped around his little finger. And it's no wonder...

He's just too cute.

All Wrapped Up

Y

is for Youth

FONT CATEGORIES

To fully understand how to differentiate and use fonts, here are seven categories into which they can be organized:

Font	Description	Examples
Serif	Technically, the serif is a little line off the end of a character, such as in Times New Roman or Garamond. Serif fonts are typically classic styles and not overly trendy. They are also very readable since many books and newspapers use serif type and our eye is used to seeing it.	**Times New Roman is a serif font** Garamond is a serif font Jackson Junior Wide is a serif font Benjamin is a serif font COPPERPLATE IS A SERIF FONT
Sans Serif	Sans, the French word for "without," literally means there are no small strokes on the letters. Sans serif text, such as Arial or Century Gothic, has a very simple and clean style often used in signs and advertisements.	Arial is a sans serif font Century Gothic is a sans serif font Bedles Wide is a sans serif font Jackson Junior Sans Wide is a sans serif font
Caps	Caps fonts use all capital letters for both upper- and lowercase letters. They are great to use for emphasis because they tend to be bold in their styling.	CASTELLAR IS A CAPS FONT FELIX TITLING IS A CAPS FONT FLOWER GARDEN IS A CAPS FONT BENJAMIN CAPS DROP IS A CAPS FONT
Script	A cursive font, such as English 111 or Kunstler Script, can add a formal or feminine flair to a page.	English 111 is a script font Kunstler Script is a script font Alyssa Black Tie is a script font Noodles is a script font
Calligraphy	These fonts are made to resemble the stylings of a professional calligrapher and can add Old World charm to your titles or journals.	Alyssa Afternoon is a calligraphy font **Mistral is a calligraphy font** Zapfino is a calligraphy font Lucida Calligraphy is a calligraphy font
Handwriting	These fonts look as if they were hand written and come in many styles including block, cursive, and child writing styles.	Meegles is a handwriting font Brina is a handwriting font Charlotte is a handwriting font Jessie is a handwriting font Bradley Hand ITC is a handwriting font
Display or Decorative	These are the unique or funky and fun typestyles that often work best for titles.	**Ryan is a decorative font** Girls Are Weird is a decorative font Love Letters is a decorative font Boys On Mopeds is a decorative font Sky Pie is a decorative font

Gardening Girl

Samantha got her very own gardening gloves this year to help mommy plant pansies. This was our very first time planting flowers at the new house, and we wanted to make our yard beautiful. Sam did such a great job!

Samantha

digging with her trowel

Very serious about watering.

APRIL 2005

RELATIONSHIP ISSUES

Renée sticks with sans serif fonts for journaling but uses fancier fonts for titles. When using several types of fonts on one page, Renée likes them to all be from the same family, or paired with very neutral, simple fonts. This is called a concordant relationship and follows a principle of "less is more" to avoid bombarding the eyes with a mess of too many complex and competing styles.

For Gardening Girl (page 15), Renée chose a fun, handwritten font for the title that really stands out and communicates the emotional tone of the photo. Had she also written her journal in this font, it would have created a very busy page that is difficult to read. Instead, she chose a toned-down, yet whimsical, font for her journal.

In S is for Summer (opposite), Renée chose a very basic sans serif font for the title—like blue jeans, it can go with anything. She chose a sweet poem typed in a feminine script for her journal.

To add more design to the page without adding another font type, try changing the size, color, or style of the same font to add contrast. In Sunkissed (page 19), Renée used capitals, bolds, and italics of just one font to create an energetic title.

MIX IT UP

Another effective technique to create contrast and emphasize words within a paragraph or list is to use color, italics, script, or even a very different font. For example, in the text below you see how the word "weeks" is emphasized from the brown text by a pink color and a script font, and "loved" is similarly highlighted using a pink, decorative font.

Even though it didn't arrive until *weeks* after Christmas, Sabrina loved her new princess and fairies sheet set.

S

is for summer

smile

Summer is a charming lass, slipping barefoot through the grass.
Rosy-cheeked windswept hair, spreading sunshine everywhere.
Up and down the fields and hills, magic colors Summer spills.
Flowers bloom so bright and gay, Beauty blesses Summer's way.

Beverly Andersson

HOW MUCH IS TOO MUCH?

Mixing and matching fonts is fun, but be careful not to have too much of a good thing. Try to use a maximum of three different fonts per layout. A general rule Renée follows is the more fonts you use, the simpler they should be. This will prevent the fonts from taking attention away from the photos.

Project Details

ALL WRAPPED UP (page 13)

Although Renée used several types of fonts in this layout—from a stenciled "Harry" to a typewriter font to a bold sans serif letter, nothing takes away from the focal point of the page: the photo of Harry wrapped up in a towel. Renée does this by keeping all of her fonts, as well as her colors, in the same family so there isn't competition for attention.

GARDENING GIRL (page 15)

Renée draws inspiration for her scrapbook layouts from everywhere, even magazine advertisements. She rips out ones she likes, or sketches a template of it, and stores them in a folder. When she's stumped on a design, Renée looks to the folder for help. In "Gardening Girl," Renée used a gridlike layout for the photos, embellishments, and text.

S IS FOR SUMMER (page 17)

S is for Summer is a perfect example of how Renée uses type, embellishments, and patterns to enhance a page and bring out the meaning behind the photo, rather than overpower it. She achieves this by adding solid blocks to break up a busy pattern, placing consistent pink fabric flower embellishments in an odd number, and using just two fonts.

SUNKISSED (opposite)

To capture a sweet moment of her daughter catching a ray of sun, Renée used warm colors to contrast with the blue-sky background of the photo. Though this page does not document a significant event, nor does the journal reveal anything earth shattering, the fine details—from the button embellishments to the definition of "smile"—enforces the idea that this special, everyday moment is worth remembering.

SUn kIssED

smile (smil) 1. to move the tips of one's mouth upward to express pleasure or happiness

Dear Olivia...
After I chose the perfect paper and title for this page I sat to think of what I wanted to say. Honestly, I just wanted to scrapbook this photo because you look so radiant and beautiful in it, and we are having a cold spell in the beginning of spring so I wanted to shake off the chill with some warm, fun colors. So really, I don't know what else to say, so I searched to find the perfect quote and I do believe I found one:

Far away there in the sunshine are my highest aspirations. I may not reach them, but I can look up and see their beauty, believe in them, and follow where they lead.

--Louisa May Alcott

Louisa May Alcott was one of my favorite authors when I was about your age (you have to read Little Women) and I found this quote so fitting of you. I know you will go far little girl, as long as you keep your eyes directed toward the sunshine.

 pets

Don't forget about the members of your family who don't talk or bring home report cards. Pets bring a lot of joy and love to a home and they deserve to be documented as part of your family history. Follow your pet around with your camera to capture their typical everyday moments, considering composition, background, and contrast as you peer into the camera's LCD or viewfinder.

Natalie Williams, an American Sign Language Interpreter from Virginia, has created special pages for her two cats, Johnna and Gus. Because they are indoor cats, the backdrop of the photos is always Natalie's home, and most often her floral bedspread. "I don't like the page to compete with the background of the photos," Natalie says, "so I often do a very simple page."

Nick Kelsh, author of *How to Photograph Your Life*, recommends when it comes to cats, wait until they climb up to a windowsill for beautiful, natural light. Also, try to fill the frame with a close up of the cat, leaving out the furniture.

Keep in mind that if you properly compose your photo when you shoot it, it will prominently feature the subject that caught your eye, and therefore require much less work with cropping when you are ready to use it in a layout.

For dogs, however, Nick has a different trick. He suggests finding a background that contrasts with your dog's color. Dark dogs should be photographed on bright backgrounds and the opposite for light or white dogs. This will help them stand out and create a striking photo.

Project Details

PUPPY LOVE
Designer Traci Turchin used wonderful close-ups of a new puppy—who even seemed to smile for the camera! —in a modern, modular design with seamless edges between the two photos. In keeping with the clean lines of her layout, she chose a sans serif font for both the title and the journaling. The journal of the potential names for the puppy was kept short at 3" (7.6 cm), with adequate spacing between the lines—called leading—for easy readability.

Puppy Puppy Puppy Love Love Love

We knew we had to take you home when
you smiled for the camera!
We'll call you...
Brandy or
Georgia or
Savannah or
Harriet or
Belle or...
Penny. That's it. Penny.

on the road

Road trip! The car is packed: You've got snacks, sunscreen, plastic dinosaurs, and, of course, your camera. Think you're set? Pick your destination and bring these photography tips along with you.

BEACH BOUND

- There are many challenges to taking photos outside on a sunny day. To avoid squinty eyes and scrunched up faces, shoot your subject sitting under an umbrella.

- Start shooting later in the day and you'll benefit from the more golden tones of the setting sun and from fewer unknown beachgoers crowding the background of your photos.

- Try to keep the horizon at the top or bottom third of the frame. If centered, it cuts the photo in half.

- When not in use, keep your camera dry and sand-free by storing it in a zippered plastic bag out of direct light.

- The beach is not just for the summer—get beautiful shots off-season of billowy clouds, large waves, scavenging seagulls, and even snow at the shore's edge.

TRIP TO THE ZOO

- Zoom, zoom, zoom. Use the zoom feature on your camera to get as close as possible to the animals and crop out any unsightly background.

- Try to be at the same level as the animal you are shooting, rather than pointing the camera downward.

- Keep shooting even if the weather is overcast; diffused light often creates beautiful shots.

- Check if the zoo offers any special events such as demonstrations or feedings. You're likely to get more exciting action shots.

- If photographing through glass, turn off your flash to reduce glare.

- Unless you're shooting for *National Geographic*, try to capture the reactions of your family or friends viewing, petting, and feeding the animals for a more personal account of your time at the zoo.

- Follow the zoo's rules to ensure you go home with great photos and all your limbs.

PARKS AND PLAYGROUNDS

- Capture the color-drenched scenery by focusing on details such as ball pits, bright slides and tunnels, murals, or a souvenir stand.

- Tell a story by documenting everything (even the tiniest, silliest details!) from the moment you leave your house to your return.

- Get in on the action by squatting at the bottom of the slide or hanging on the monkey bars.

- Take photos of the photo taker! To get pictures of the whole clan, pass the camera around, use the self-timer, or ask strangers to snap a shot or two.

Life's a Beach!

Daddy, some shades and the surf...what else could a girl ask for? A popsicle couldn't hurt.

Zoo trip

Sam was just learing to walk with confidence when we took her to the zoo for the day. She loved all the animals (pink flamingos were the favorite purely for being pink). We loved watching her walk and even run around, gripping tightly to her stuffed tiger the whole way.

Project Details

LIFE'S A BEACH (page 23)

Using different fonts is one way to add design to your text; shaping your text is another. This title "Life's a Beach" is shaped into a wave, an appropriate design element for the subject of the page. Even though computer printers can't print white, the text in this layout will work because it's layered on colored backgrounds and printed on white paper. The photos capture the beachgoers up close and in action digging or walking. The photo from behind ensures the pose is natural and fully engaged in the elements.

ZOO TRIP (pages 24–25)

Leading is the space between the lines of text. In a journaling block, you'll always want a fair amount of leading to make the text easy to read. For titles, however, overlapping words like "Zoo" and "Trip" can create a unique design when the words are in different colors. The large photo is set to bleed all the way to the edge for a dramatic start to the page. The inset photo stands out because it is in a frame. The black background makes the photos and text seem to pop off the page.

A PARK OUTING (opposite)

Text alignment refers to how the rows of text are lined up: right, left, or centered. Full justification means the letters are lined up both on the right and left side. This creates a neat, typeset style to the page. In "A Park Outing," the journal takes on the same even, modular design as the rest of the elements. This layout uses a wide selection of photos to tell a story about the day. Setting the photos into the layout in different sizes and orientations (portrait and landscape) helps add variety.

Nana and I have the best time at Brookdale Park. We go on the squiggly slide together, Nana pushes me in the swings and always helps me on the monkey bars. Nana thinks I'm part monkey and part mole since I also like to race through the tunnel Hold onto my hat!

A Park Outing

▣ silly

Kathy O'Brien's seven-year-old son has a thing for giraffes. So when he saw a six-foot (1.8 m) stuffed giraffe in a toy store, he knew had to have it. The only problem: it was $99. Kathy explained to him that if he really wanted it, he'd have to save up by doing chores around the house. Six months later, after earning his 99th dollar, he was finally able to purchase his beloved giraffe.

"The whole time we had been taking photos—one of the first time he saw the giraffe, a picture of him handing over the money, the reaction of the staff that this little seven-year-old could save $99, and him unwrapping it when he got home. I also saved the receipt so I could put it all in a scrapbook page," said Kathy. "I was able to tell this story from A to Z, and I think this is one he might want to tell his kids one day."

OLIVE FOR THE MOMENT

Renée's scrapbook pages of the silly things her four-year-old does will give him plenty to look back on. "What kid doesn't put olives on his fingers?" Renée asks. "What's special about this page is how Harry's personality really came through in these photos."

Another reason these silly pictures made it into a scrapbook: "In a year he might not even like olives anymore. I have to capture these memories while I can," Renée explains.

As for Harry's addiction to chocolate milk, Renée thinks that's going to last forever. "He's a real addict, and he just looked so darn cute in the photos," says Renée. "I want us to look at these pages in twenty years and say either 'Do you remember how much you loved chocolate milk?' or 'Do you believe after twenty years you still drink chocolate milk?'"

Project Details

OLIVE FINGERS

Renée captured Harry's silliness in three close-up shots and made them the focal point of the page. The photos each show a stage in an action sequence, which is a very effective way to tell a story at a glance. For the titles and journals, she mixed several different simple fonts and wrote her thoughts in sentence fragments to complement the spontaneous theme of the page. She also hung tags with mini-messages on them to accent the page.

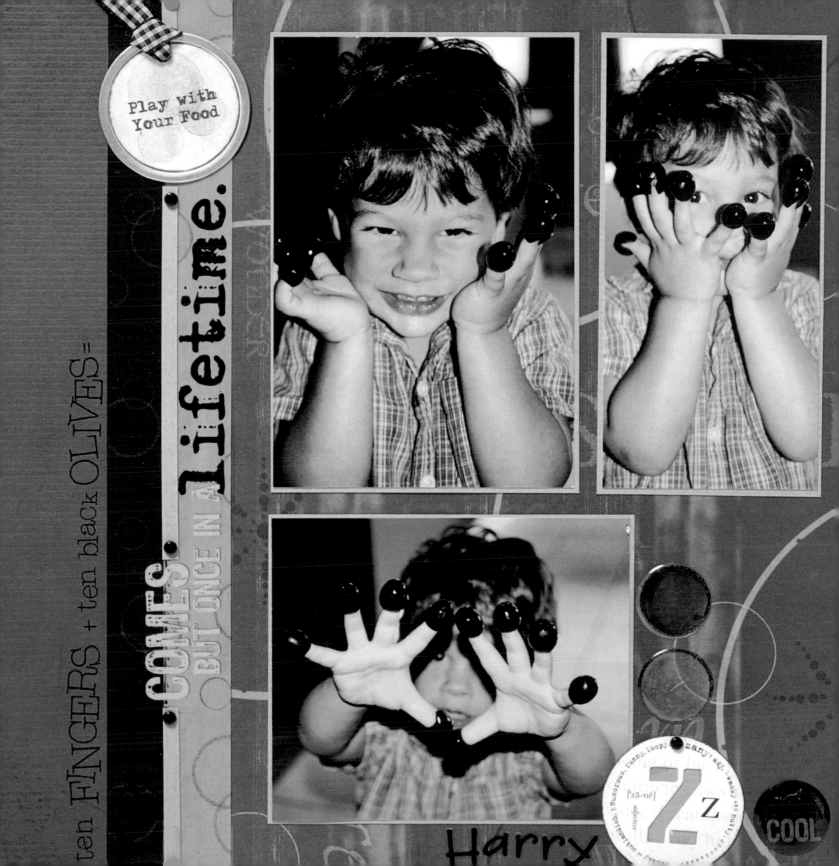

Play with Your Food

ten FINGERS + ten black OLIVES = COMES BUT ONCE IN A lifetime.

Harry

Z z
[zā-nē]

COOL

HAIL TO THE FONT QUEEN

Most children will have report cards, birthday party photos, and yearbooks to look back on for reminiscing. But it takes a scrapbook to remember the day they decided to cut their sister's hair with pinking shears or spent hours running through a lawn sprinkler.

Of course, each silly moment warrants a perfect font. Maryellen Young, known by her screen name to her scrapbook friends as the Font Queen, keeps a large collection of fonts just for this purpose.

"I am always on the lookout for a new font—and when I come across one that I like and do not have in my collection, I go on the hunt to find a way to acquire it for my very own," she says. "Some people collect spoons, I collect fonts." You can grow your own font collection by purchasing software or font collections on a CD or by downloading them from the Internet.

To download a font from the Internet, look for TrueType versions because they will work with the most software. Click the font file and save to your computer. If the file is a .zip, uncompress it to extract the original file. Once extracted, the file should be .ttf. Click the Windows Start menu and choose Settings, Control Panel, then Fonts to open the Fonts folder. Click on the File menu and choose Install New Font. Click on the folder C:\ in the bottom-left of the install new font window and you will see your new font appear as a selection choice in the top-left of the window. Click on your new font and click OK to install.

Project Details

CHOCOLATE MILK (opposite)

Renée used preprinted paper with a chocolate theme to showcase Harry's Ovaltine addiction. You could create this look using a variety of fonts and phrases with different curves and rotations. Renée matches the distressed style of the paper by using a typewriter-style font for her journal on tea-stained paper. The photos are set semi-overlapping for a less formal look, and the photo borders match the journal border.

 Insert the bonus disk to download five original Mountaincow fonts.

"Cwalk-kit milk peas?"

Several times a day, Harry goes through the pantry and comes out with his beloved container of Ovaltine. He's the only kid in our family who didn't give up milk when he gave up the bottle. Chocolate milk must be drunk from his mickey mouse cup and Mommy must rinse out the straw first (even though it is clean already) otherwise the milk is deemed 'yucky'. When Harry feels the need for an extra kick he'll ask for coffee-milk, or better yet, chocolate coffee-milk. (yes, I'm to blame for his love of coffee). I don't care really, as long as he drinks his milk!

time for a drink

CHOCOLAT "SOLUBIA"

CHOCOLATS
91, Rue de Rivoli
CCURSALE: 9, Boul

Hors Concours
aux Expositions

CHOCOLAT GUÉRIN-BOUTRON
CHOCOLAT GUÉRIN

550 Célébrités éditées pour le

CHOCOLAT
RE D'OR

Eggs
Candy
Bunnies
Dresses
Blooming
Chocolate
Hunts
Church
Jelly Beans

Easter
egg hunt

YOUR MOTHER GOT
CARRIED AWAY WITH THE
MATCHING TRUNKS, BUT THEY
HELP ME TO REMEMBER MY
BEAUTIFUL BOYS ON
A PERFECT FATHER'S DAY.

father
& son

OF ALL THE PHOTOS WE
HAVE, THIS ONE STILL FEELS
LIKE YESTERDAY.

YOUR MOTHER GOT
CARRIED AWAY WITH THE
MATCHING TRUNKS, BUT THEY
HELP ME TO REMEMBER MY
BEAUTIFUL BOYS ON
A PERFECT FATHER'S DAY.

East
egg

chapter 2

for the holidays

In between present buying, costume making, egg decorating, and cookie baking, holiday traditions are made. And chances are that what ends up on film doesn't tell the full story. Narrating the holidays through journaling is essential to differentiate the magic between years. Don't forget to document the *who* (the guest list), the *what* (dressing up like Batman…again), the *where* (your first home), the *when* (the great blizzard on Easter), the *why* (Santa's surprises), and the *how* (everyone carrying the tree into the house).

winter

"Scrapbooking the holidays can be a little repetitive," says Renée Foss, an award-winning scrapbook designer. "You've got photos of the kids opening presents. A photo of the tree. You've got red and green."

Fellow designer Traci Turchin feels the same way. "If you're twenty years old, you have twenty Christmases!" she says.

So how do you keep your holiday layouts unique and special?

"Find a new angle," suggests Traci. "Instead of just what we did on Christmas day, I will focus on a tiny detail that made this particular Christmas different." For example, Traci did a page on the special Swedish Cream Cookies her grandmother makes every year. In the past, her grandfather's role was to pipe the cream filling. Since he just passed away, Traci and her sister helped their grandmother this year. "This page was about missing my grandfather and how nice it felt for my sister and me to help," Traci says.

Renée keeps her layouts fresh by focusing on how her kids change from year to year. "I enjoy taking the kids' holiday portrait to see how they've grown since the last Christmas."

To do that, Renée stocks up on rolls and rolls of film and snaps away at her two sons and daughter, individually and all together. She'll choose one photo for the traditional holiday card and uses the many leftovers for scrapbook pages. She fell in love with a series of photos of her youngest son in a Santa hat and created a page titled "Santa Baby." Never part with photos that you love, even if they weren't used for the reason you took them.

Renée took her favorite photo from a sequence and made it the largest on the layout. "The two smaller ones showed different expressions, so I wanted to include those, too."

By using her home printer, Renée was able to print the exact size of the photo she wanted instead of being restricted to standard photo sizes. She made the rest of the layout using preprinted paper, velvet ribbon, letter stamps, and store-bought embellishments.

"I love texture, so I used the velvet ribbon almost as an arrow to the large photo," says Renée. For more shimmer, Renée used gold paint on the title, which she hand-cut.

Santa Baby

HARRY, 3 YEARS OLD
CHRISTMAS PHOTO SHOOT, 2004

This same project can be made quickly and easily on the computer with a very similar outcome, even if you are not (yet) a Hall of Fame scrapbook page designer. For complete directions, see The Projects section on page 40.

Another way Renée keeps her holiday layouts from being repetitive is by using a variation of traditional colors. In "Santa Baby," Renée chose a deep burgundy with subtle patterns as her background and then accented with gold.

There is no rule that Christmas pages must be red and green. Using rich blues, purples, and metallics such as gold and silver will create a festive page. Use your photos as a guide for what colors work best. Renée has determined a color scheme for a page about Christmas morning by matching the paper to her children's pajamas.

For Renée's traditional holiday portrait spread (pages 38–39), instead of kelly green, she chose a combination of moss and olive green with red accents and metal embellishments. For added dimension, Renée ripped the edge of the paper before layering it and used a vellum envelope to hold the actual holiday card her family sent out that Christmas season.

While she does include some journaling on the left-hand page about the photo shoot, Renée also tucks the family update letter—which she sends with the holiday card—into the envelope on the right-hand page. This is one of the ways she can add more journaling to a page.

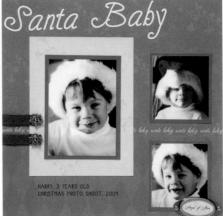

TRUTH IN JOURNALING

They way you journal may be as personal as the journals themselves. For some scrapbookers, the journal is the very last element on a page, written when all else has been laid out.

"I often write the journal after I've laid everything out. If there's no room I get creative and add a pocket," says Renée.

Otherwise, Renée will use her computer to create a journal that will fit on her layout. "I don't hand-journal, not because I don't like my handwriting but because I am analytical. I'm a chemist so I like everything to be lined up. If I write it on my computer, I know I can make it the exact size I want it."

But just because Renée's journals are typed doesn't mean they are perfect. "I don't even spell check or re-read my journals before I print them. I figure if I wrote it, it's what I meant to say—so if you see any typos, that's why."

Renée calls her journaling process "unelegant but real." "For a while, journals were very flowery, emotional, and dramatic. And then I asked, 'Whose kids are that perfect? Whose marriage is that great?' I'm all for warts and journaling. If I am mad at my daughter, I might create a page about what happened at that point and why I still love her."

One example is of a page Renée made about how her husband is able to "distract and divert" when their youngest is on the verge of a tantrum. Amid photos of the father and son, Renée writes:

(Top left) Created using traditional scrapbooking techniques *(Top right)* Created using scrapbooking software

Here we see Daddy employing the age-old technique of "distract and divert" with Harry. These photos (opposite), were taken only moments after Harry started to have a minor snit fit. Daddy quickly swooped in and tickled the little whiner [distract] and then started to toss Harry up and down and greet him with a kiss [diversion]. The frown was quickly turned upside down and we were able to avoid a major meltdown. If this could only be as effective on the other two kids...

Rachel Schleich, a teacher from Pennsylvania, has a slightly different approach to journaling. She uses her computer, too, but that's only her first step.

"I journal on my computer because I tend to write a lot and this is a great way for me to organize my thoughts and tell a coherent story," says Rachel. "Then I handwrite it into the album because it's more personal. This way when my daughter is reading a story about her it won't seem so cold, it will seem like mom is telling it to her."

This process also helps Rachel figure out how much space she needs in her layout for her journals.

GETTING STARTED

No matter what step in your scrapbooking process journaling happens, actually putting words to paper can be the hardest part.

Linda C. Senn, author of *The Many Faces of Journaling*, suggests taking a long look at your photographs, closing your eyes, and reliving that moment. "Run a movie through your mind, see the movement, feel the hugs. If you relive it in your mind, your journals will have more life to them," she says.

Use the five senses as a checklist when describing a person or event. "Did Grandmother smell like lavender or cinnamon? Adding smell, sound, touch, and taste are powerful ways to enhance a scrapbook entry," says Linda.

Another trick to get started is to write as though your journal is your dearest friend and confidante. Pretend as though you are talking or writing an email and don't worry about using full sentences. Using phrases and fragments will be more like your voice.

WHAT'S THE STORY?

For Traci, her layouts are all about the journaling. "I consider my scrapbook style to be 'story-centered.' I always try to keep my stories at the center of the layout because that's the most important thing to me," she says.

Traci always journals first, and if all she has is a napkin to write on when she's inspired, that's what she'll use. "I always go back and retype my journal. Then I heavily edit it so it's saying exactly what I want it to say."

Traci's secret to journaling: practice. "Anyone really serious about improving their journals should practice. The more you write, the easier it is to find your voice."

Use a journal to keep track of daily events. Chances are, you won't have the time to create a page right when the event happens.

Looking for the perfect

Christmas Photo

One roll black and white film.
One roll color film.
One new dress.
One uncooperative baby.
Ten minutes.
Voila! The perfect photo for our cards!
I was tired of doing the professional portrait
routine for our Christmas cards so I decided again
to do it myself. I couldn't have been happier with
the results!

HARrY

OLiViA

SAM

The final result.

🎄

Perfect!

HAPPY HOLIDAYS!
ROB, RENEE
OLIVIA, SAM AND HARRY

Write the journal while the experience is fresh in your head, then refer back to your journal once you've developed your photos and are ready to build a page. By keeping a daily journal, you'll find your groove and be more comfortable with your writing.

Once Traci has her journals done, she focuses on her photos, spending time on her computer to make sure they are cropped to the best angle and size and the colors are perfect.

Her next step is to sketch a design with pen and paper and then translate it onto her computer. For "Christmas Princess" (opposite), Traci was inspired by the candy-cane pattern she used to trim her photos.

"Those candy canes just embody what's playful and fun about Christmas, and they matched the photos in both mood and color. So I was motivated by the candy canes and started with those," Traci says.

If you find yourself inspired by a single embellishment or pattern, find photos or memorabilia that have the same theme or feel. If you have a sophisticated embellishment with beads, you will probably want your photos to be just as special. Use your whimsical stickers with your cuter photos.

Traci then took the three photos of the little girl in a red coat and lined them up, edge to edge. Since the photos were similar in format and content, arranging them in this way helps them look unified and sequential instead of just repetitive. This technique lets you work with the photos instead of having them work against you. It's also a great way to use a lot of photos on one page.

Project Details

SANTA BABY (page 35)

Mixing background patterns, like the floral and harlequin ones here, can work beautifully if the scale and colors of the patterns don't compete with one another. For more information about creating your own patterns, see page 119. If you're using a patterned background, use solid-colored mats behind your photos to help bring attention to your photos. Print your own solid colors to ensure everything matches with your borders, patterns, and text colors.

You can also mix fonts, such as a script title and block letter journaling. Vary your titles by printing them at angles. For more information about text styles, see chapter 1.

To add a ribbon, place it with double-stick tape and secure with a decorative brad. The metal bookplate was secured to the bottom right corner with brads.

HOLIDAY PORTRAIT (pages 38–39)

Choose a palette of colors to unify a spread. In this case, Renée used olive green and tan with an accent of red. The left-hand page used a patterned background, so the photos were matted on solid colors. These photos were taken with black-and-white film, but you can achieve the same effect with color photos by using your computer to convert the photos to grayscale.

To add texture to the page, Renée added metal embellishments sparingly and tore the edge of a layer for an added dimension. Choosing embellishments made of the same material—from the photo corners to the little letters and Christmas trees—enhances the layout instead of overpowering it. For more information about embellishments, see chapter 6.

CHRISTMAS PRINCESS (opposite)

Lining up similar photos from the same photo session edge to edge can be a very powerful way to display a series of emotions or add motion to your page. To unify photos that are lined up edge to edge, create one border or photo mat for all the photos.

Flipping a pattern—to make it go in a different direction— as seen here with the candy canes is a great way to add visual variety while keeping design elements consistent.

Shaping your titles into waves or circles can really make your layouts stand apart. Traci made this title into a wave to add movement to an otherwise very symmetrical page. For more about curved text, see page 117.

You're such a big girl in your red pea coat! You look like such a little angel, maybe we'll put you on top of the tree?

spring

The first St. Patrick's Day Kelly Lynch spent in New York City, she did everything typical to the holiday. "I had friends from Texas come to visit so we had a very New York day. We went to St. Patrick's Cathedral. We saw the parade. We did a pub crawl," says Kelly. "I picked up a lot of memorabilia like matchbooks from all the bars we went to and postcards of the cathedral. Anything 'scrap-able.'"

MAKE A LIST, CHECK IT TWICE

One of Kelly's missions for her scrapbook pages is to show she's "been there, done that." An effective way to journal about a series of events is to simply list them. For an action-packed day such as Kelly's, you can even make an agenda with the times of all the activities to show just how much was accomplished in twenty-four hours. This way you can include everything you did, even if you don't have photos for everything.

Lists are also a fantastic way to get your feelings down on paper. "Goals are the perfect thing to list," says Linda. "Range from practical to emotional. Cover business, home, and personal goals. Make some modest and some outrageous."

Other list ideas include: The top ten books you read or movies you saw over the year; friends and how they helped you this year; the five things you fear the most and why.

Lists don't have to be written in the typical grocery manner. Sprinkle words all over your page, or create one journal box with each item in a different font. Justify the text so it's one block and then layer an image over it so the words act as a frame.

In the "Easter Egg Hunt" layout, a list of all things Easter is written in transparent text. Transparent text is a subtle way to embellish a page. It allows you to add journaling in a very soft, whisperlike way. It's not as obvious as opaque text but it will still be eye-catching.

Traci separated the large photo and the list journal from the rest of the page with a thin strip filled with a green and white floral pattern. Since it was such a small area, the small flowers packed a punch and created a nice border to the photo. She then used the same pattern to fill the letters of the word "Easter" in the title, but altered the scale so the flowers were larger. This way, the letters didn't appear too busy and overwhelm the layout. Being able to adjust the scale of patterns makes them more versatile. If tiny flowers make a page too busy, you can adjust the size of the flowers so they work with your layout. For more information about using patterns, see chapter 3.

Project Details

EASTER EGG HUNT

Set the mood of a page by using a scenery shot as a background image. Traci used this photo of a little girl gathering Easter eggs as a colorful and sweet way to tell the story of her Easter celebration. Then she added a close up so we can see her smile and her basketful of eggs.

It's important to keep readability in mind when using pattern-filled text. Adding a contrasting outline color may help the letters stand out and make a title easier to read. Also consider making just one word of your title patterned, and use a complementary color for the rest of the title.

By using transparent text for the journal, you won't overpower your title. Readability is also important here. You're looking for just the right percentage of transparency so you can easily read the text. Do a test print to make sure you haven't made it too light or used too pale a background.

Eggs
Candy
Bunnies
Dresses
Blooming
Chocolate
Hunts
Church
Jelly Beans

Easter
egg hunt

summer

If Father's Day is all about Dad, why doesn't he contribute to the scrapbook page about his day? Chances are, if you're the only one in your household who creates scrapbooks, all the journaling is from your perspective. This may set a nice, consistent tone for all your scrapbooks, but having others contribute their voices will help complete your family legacy.

"Make it a family project," suggests Linda C. Senn, author of *The Many Faces of Journaling*. "Pave the way and have a few things done so no one is going at a project cold. That can be overwhelming." If you ask a family member to contribute to a scrapbook page, give them an option of dictating to a tape recorder or a younger person in the family. "That within itself enhances family bonding," Linda points out.

Want to inspire others to contribute to your scrapbook? Here are some tips:

• **Create a questionnaire.** This will serve as a guide for your family members' contributions. Ask loose, open-ended questions such as "Who were your best friends growing up?" You can also ask more pointed questions such as "What Easter traditions did you like best?"

• **Look at what's not in the photo.** A picture can show ages, fashions, and locations, but what's not being shown that you remember? Was it record high temperatures? Did you just find out you were expecting? Ask your family members what they remember.

• **Where were you when...** Record your version of history. A resident of St. Louis, Linda vividly remembers driving home from an eye doctor appointment with her son when the Cardinals clinched the World Series. "It's just a fun little memory of hearing it on the radio and watching the whole city cheer. I'd never find that in a history book," says Linda. "Another way to do this is to sit in front of the news and just track your reactions to what's going on."

• **Look for a few good pens.** Capture your family's handwriting. If they prefer to type, get their signature for posterity. Also, use a proper archival pen to ensure the writing lasts.

Project Details

FATHER'S DAY

When you're using one strong photo for a page layout, crop it to accentuate its strengths. In the photo of a father with his boys, it appears they are looking out at the deep blue of the ocean against the light blue of the sky. By cropping out the other beachgoers on the right and the extra sand at the bottom, you can extend the photo to take up the entire left side of the page for a dramatic impact.

By using short stripes, you can add more color and contrast to a design. If you want a more subtle touch of color, rotate your stripes to be in the same direction as the length of your shape. For example, if you have a tall, thin rectangle going from the top of your page to the bottom, use horizontal stripes for a strong impact and vertical stripes for something more subdued.

father
& sons

OF ALL THE PHOTOS WE HAVE, THIS ONE STILL FEELS LIKE YESTERDAY.

YOUR MOTHER GOT CARRIED AWAY WITH THE MATCHING TRUNKS, BUT THEY HELP ME TO REMEMBER MY BEAUTIFUL BOYS ON A PERFECT FATHER'S DAY.

autumn

Sometimes, how you actually spend the holiday won't end up in the scrapbook, but something more unexpected will. Lisa Corso, of Syracuse, New York, loves to play pranks. One autumn day, she and her husband decided to have some fun with their neighbors, so they created a scarecrow—of sorts—for their front lawn. Manny (the name they gave him) was leaning over with his jeans falling down, revealing a pumpkin moon to the neighborhood.

"It was so silly and our neighbors had a laugh about it," says Lisa. "Then I realized we had fifty or sixty cars drive by a day, with some people stopping to take pictures of Manny the Mooning Pumpkin! Then to top it all off, Manny was in the local newspaper."

Lisa quickly ran out to get several copies of the newspaper and one is dog-eared for her scrapbook. "There are just some things you know you want to document. This is more monumental than the annual hayride photos."

TRUE AUTUMN
Autumn holiday pages can be a pleasure to design since the photos are rich with oranges, browns, and greens. Traci was drawn to this picture of two boys sitting on pumpkins because of the vibrant colors and even composition. "I love photos that are traditionally seasonal, ones that remind you of all that's great about pumpkins," says Traci.

Traci knew orange would be a central color in the page. She then chose a green title and accents to play off the blue sky. Since people read from upper left to bottom right, Traci added a little accent to the bottom right corner to bring the eye back into the page. In this case, the branch works as an arrow back to the photo of the boys on the pumpkins.

Project Details

PICKING PUMPKINS
This project uses a combination of techniques discussed throughout the chapter. One striking photo takes up most of the page, putting the viewer in the pumpkin patch with the little boys. A well-defined color scheme centered on the strikingly orange pumpkins sets the palette for the page. Short horizontal lines make a strong separation between the photo and the journaling. One word of the title is partially transparent so it can layer over the other word.

❊ Insert the Bonus CD for the Halloween Gallery how-to video for more spooky layout ideas.

Picking pumpkins

I'm still in shock we captured one photo of Dean and Keith sitting still at the pumpkin patch. From the minute they stepped out of the car, they raced around the pumpkin patch like the ghost of Halloween was chasing them! Luckily, these two perfectly-sized pumpkins gave them a chance to rest.

Mount
Snow

We had one of those rare perfect East Coast ski days. The sun was shining, it wasn't freezing, and we had actual powder! It was by far one of the most perfect days we'd ever had, and it was so great that we were all together to enjoy it. Best moment of the day: beers on the deck after the last run!

pipe

dreams

Our African Adventure

On the third day of our vacation to Africa we were able to take an African Safari tour by Kunto, a member of a nearby African tribe. We saw so many animals and each one seemed closer than the next. Our drive ended with a beautiful sunset and the most graceful giraffe I have ever seen. I was so happy to capture the true beauty of Africa on film so that my memories of the trip could be shared for years to come.

dreams

chapter 3

for the traveler

Vacations, whether down at the shore or across the country, provide invaluable memories and keepsakes. Add the local flavor of your destination to your pages by capturing and featuring the patterns inherent in the location, from porch awning stripes to leopard spots.

warm

When Colleen Mahoney returned from her two sons' first trip to Disney, she didn't rush to put together her album. "This was an important album," says Colleen. "I wanted it to be done right so I really planned out how every photo was going to be used. I think I spent two months just shopping for the right supplies!"

The entire book is a labor of love, complete with homemade shaker boxes, but her whole family agrees on which spread they love to look at. Colleen made a page titled "Our five favorite things to do at Disney" and used wallet-sized photos to illustrate them.

"One of the 'favorites' is our trip to the water park and the photo is of both of the boys with their arms up as they flew down a water ride. They love taking out the album and looking at that page," says Colleen. "They get so excited and say, 'Mommy, I remember falling into the water!'"

SENSING A PATTERN

Colleen loves using patterns in her layouts but doesn't choose them until she knows what photos she's using. This way she can tie the theme of the page to her pattern. For instance, her "Bug's Life" page is laid out on leaf-patterned paper.

Patterns are a wonderful way to not only carry out a theme, but also add energy, texture, and movement to a page. When using a pattern, don't only think about the colors and the shapes being repeated. You should also consider the scale of the pattern, meaning the size of the shapes being used. The same pattern will look more or less striking or subtle depending on how large the

daisies, polka dots, stripes, or paisleys are on the page. In general, use large-scaled patterns in backgrounds and shapes, and use small-scaled patterns in frames and text.

To instantly convey a sunny and tropical travel pages, chose an appropriate pattern. The "Baby in Paradise" layout on page 52 uses a bright floral pattern is used as a background. In addition to making the title readable, a solid pink block is added to help break up the busy pattern so it doesn't overwhelm the photos.

The whimsical pattern is perfect for the subject of this page. Keep the tone of the photos in mind when choosing a pattern.

❋ See the Bonus CD for a how-to video, Mat Photos without Measuring.

WORD PLAY

Patterns don't always have to be flowers, stripes, or polka dots. Broaden the meaning of patterns by including a page from a phone book, a road map, or even a dictionary entry—anything that has repetition or consistency. For this page about a not-so-sunny trip to Florida, designer Renée Foss typed a block of text on a tag for a pattern.

The natural background paper is also a type of pattern. Consider using a close-up shot of a lemon peel, snakeskin, your lawn, or a wicker chair to create interesting patterns from nature to add to your layouts.

Project Details

NOT SO SUNNY FLORIDA
(opposite)
To really get the feeling of a damp, muddy vacation, Renée chose an earthy pattern for the background page. The greens in the photos added a nice brightness to draw attention to the cute subjects in them. The smaller scale of the pattern in the background helps to highlight the photos.

BABY IN PARADISE
(pages 52–53)
An eye-catching pattern can be just that—potentially drawing attention away from your photographs. When using powerful designs such as large flowers or polka dots, consider adding large blocks of solid colors to subdue busy patterns, and limit the areas in which the patterns are used. The larger scale of the pattern makes it as much a visual feature of the page as the photos and text.

NOT SO SUNNY FLORIDA

together (too·geth'ər, tə-) adv.

travel

We went to visit
Granny
just before Christmas
and it rained every
single day. The kids
didn't care and had a
great time as we
scrambled to find fun
things to do in cold,
rainy weather. We
had to wash all our
clothes every night,
but we had fun!

rainy adventure

Baby in paradise

From the moment we arrived at the airport, you were in heaven! You loved the flowers, the sun, everything!

aloha

fun in the water

We were much more nervous about your first experience snorkeling than you were. You jumped right in!

■ cold

The photos from Billie Sue Woolley's annual family ski trip don't vary much from year to year. "My children are grown so they're not going to replace their ski clothes often, so each year I have the same photos of the same people in the same clothes waiting for the ski lift," she laughs.

The family law attorney from Lexington, Kentucky, has found a way to distinguish each trip with a little advance planning, however. "Of course I get photos of anything different we do, such as taking a group shot in front of wherever we stay," says Billie Sue. "But I have found my travel albums come out the best when I plan ahead of time what photos I want. You have to think before you go, 'What shots do I want?'"

Several years ago, her fifteen-year-old son went skiing with friends and when he came home, he had tons of pictures of the guys hanging out, but not one of the slopes. "It was fun to see the end of the day pictures, when everyone is worn out, has a little sun on their face, and has hair going every which way," Billie Sue says. She made a mental note to get some casual end-of-the-day shots on her own next trip.

BACKGROUND CHECK
Billie Sue always includes a trail map of the ski resort in her scrapbook. Sometimes she keeps it folded and creates a pocket for it to slip into. If she's worried about the map's archival quality, she'll find it online and print it on her acid-free cardstock. "This way you can use it as a background and put your close-ups on top of it," she recommends.

Billie Sue has also used her scenery photos of mountains or snow-covered pines as a background to the photographs of her family. "This can work with any trip. For a recent trip to Las Vegas, I took a photo of the unbelievable seasonal decor at our hotel. When I enlarged the photo it was a little fuzzy, but it worked great as a background shot." You can use your image software's blur tool to create this fuzzy background look with any photo.

THAT'S THE TICKET
Lift tickets are also a great memento to add to a ski trip page since they often have the logo of the resort and the date of the trip. If the wire attachment poses a challenge or you're concerned about the archival quality of the paper, scan the lift ticket and print on acid-free paper.

GONE PLAID
For Billie Sue's quieter pages without maps or tickets, a plaid-patterned accent adds just enough design and color without being too feminine. For gender-neutral patterns, look to stripes and grids in the blue and green family.

Project Details
MOUNT SNOW
Photos of ski trips are often matted on dark blue or black backgrounds to offset the white snow. Also, ski gear is often dark and will coordinate with these colors. The subtle harlequin pattern on the bottom half of the page adds some movement to the layout. A reference to how expert ski trails are rated by diamonds is highlighted with two diamond-shaped text boxes flanking the bottom photo.

Mount Snow

We had one of those rare perfect East Coast ski days. The sun was shining, it wasn't freezing, and we had actual powder! It was by far one of the most perfect days we'd ever had, and it was so great that we were all together to enjoy it. Best moment of the day: beers on the deck after the last run!

pipe

dreams

near

Dawn Ashby's two sons have been involved with Boy Scouts for six years, but she's only been scrapbooking for three, so the only way she can catch up and continue to document all their trips and achievements is to have the boys help. "They're very involved in my memory keeping," says the mother of four. "When I am with them they'll say 'Mom, want a picture of that?'"

The most essential job the boys have is to journal about their trips. "Inevitably, one of them will have forgotten to pack an extra pair of socks so they'll write about how their feet were soaked, or just how they had fun rock climbing, or simply who is in their troop."

MAKING YOUR OWN BACKGROUND NOISE

Designer Renée Foss used a very subtle pattern for half of her background of her son's camping trip layout. In keeping with the masculine and outdoorsy style of the page, the pattern Renée chose is a mélange of words describing the outing. To create your own pattern of words and phrases, overlap text boxes where the writing has been made transparent. By lowering the opacity value, the text will appear sheer and create a nice overlapping design when layered.

Project Details

PLAYING WITH FIRE

When you're sick of solids and can't seem to find the right pattern for your layout, make your own! There are endless options when using Mountaincow's scrapbook software's pattern creator in which you can manipulate shapes, colors, and sizes or import graphics. Photograph a texture or scan in an antique parchment for a base pattern and then recolor it to match the background you want. Add dimension to your journal boxes by changing their shape or the qualities of the text inside them. See the Tips and Techniques chapter for more information on the pattern creator and journal boxes.

WHAT IS HE dOING?!?!?

FiRE STArTeR

LIVE
dangerously

Playing
with fire

What was Rob thinking when he took these photos??
It's bad enough that he allowed Harry to poke the
bonfire at the Boys Scout family campout with a stick
but to take photographic proof of the deed??
Obviously, Mom wasn't around for this particular
camping trip...only a Dad would allow a three year old
child to play with fire. Honestly, I can't figure out
what is dumber--letting Harry stir up the flames or
taking pictures him doing it. Rob assures me that the
fire that appears to be directly under Harry's foot in
the photo in reality was several feet in front of
Harry. Sigh. Looks like I'll be going camping next
time....

far

Rebecca Dohndt's scrapbook of her trip to Japan includes more than just mementos she picked up along the way. Her souvenirs serve not just as trinkets; they add special Far East details that convey the uniqueness of the experience. For instance, Rebecca fell in love with the origami paper and bought plenty of it to mat all her photos. She also had the friends she was visiting help her write the symbols of the name of the town where they stayed. She included a Japanese calendar with the dates of her visit circled, and a photo of her taking part in a prayer ceremony along with the blessing she received.

CULTURE CLUB

To convey the culture of the places you travel, find patterns in the materials you encountered, such as subway tiles, the skin of indigenous animals, or, most commonly, the fashions people wear. For items that are hard to scrapbook, like the tile or animal hide, take a close-up photo and use it as an accent on the page. For clothes such as kimonos, saris, or Irish cable knits, try placing them on your scanner to create a distinct digital pattern to import into your layout.

Project Details

OUR AFRICAN ADVENTURE

The animals and scenery of this safari are so striking, designer Ursula Page added only a hint of a striped, wavy zebra pattern to this layout. Sticking with the orange and tan of the sunset landscape photo, this monochromatic layout conveys a tranquil and peaceful quality that predominantly features the animals and the setting. A single small photo depicts the safari travelers as mere visitors among nature.

Our African Adventure

On the third day of our vacation to Africa we were able to take an African Safari tour by Kunto, a member of a nearby African tribe. We saw so many animals and each one seemed closer than the next. Our drive ended with a beautiful sunset and the most graceful giraffe I have ever seen. I was so happy to capture the true beauty of Africa on film so that my memories of the trip could be shared ✵ for years to come. ✵

Hawaii

OUR
HONEYMOON

Just
the
Girls

another day in Paradise

OUR
HONEYMOON

chapter 4

for the bride and groom

Some brides meticulously record and color-code every planning note in a three-ring binder; others hold the catering menus and fabric swatches in a battered manila envelope. Either way, from the proposal to the honeymoon, the cameras are out for a well-documented union. Armed with photos and memorabilia, all brides, mothers, and maids of honor can create sentimental records of the start of a marriage.

planning a wedding

Finding materials for a scrapbook page of the wedding planning process is fairly easy, since brides need to hold on to samples and swatches to make decisions. "Brides should bring their cameras with them everywhere, from the florist to the hair trial to the dressmaker," says wedding expert Anne Chertoff.

"This way she knows how she decided to wear her hair, but then after the wedding she can use the photos for a scrapbook. You can document the evolution of how you settled on a centerpiece, or how you chose your cake."

Don't fret, however, if the photos of your china from the department store or the half-eaten slice of cake you and your fiancé devoured aren't as wonderful as the feeling you had when you were there. Chances are, the lighting wasn't great, your hair wasn't perfect, and there are strangers in the background.

By using your computer to scrapbook, you can digitally enhance your photographs. Tools that crop, recolor, or brighten can save photos that might otherwise be bound for the trash.

When Alison Rosenthal, a college consultant in New York, shopped for a wedding dress, it was a family affair. "It's not that typical for a dad to come along, but I don't have a typical dad. He loves to be part of all the big events and he only has daughters, but he also just loves to shop. He bought my husband his tuxedo!" she laughs. The photos of her trying on her dress, inspecting it in the mirror, and trying out a veil were adorable, but had an unfortunate yellow tint from the fluorescent lighting of the dressing room.

To salvage the photos, designer Traci Turchin converted them to grayscale. Not only did the yellow tint go away but also the photos were made more dramatic and Alison's white dress stood out as the central story of the page. Instead of focusing on the glare of the lights, all eyes are drawn to the bride-to-be's smile.

QUICK FIXES FOR PHOTOS

Rotate: Use this tool to change landscape photos to portrait or vice versa.

Flip: Want to have someone facing into a page? Have them cooperate by flipping the photo. This is also a great tool when repeating a photo or image to create a pattern.

Crop: Trim away edges of the photo you don't want.

Recolor: Adjust the hue of your image to give your photo an allover new color. The Match RGB button will adjust the hue, brightness, and saturation values to recolor an image to match an RGB color value.

Tint: This will first change your photo to grayscale before recoloring for a more even colorful effect.

Brightness: The higher the value of your photo's brightness, the lighter it will appear. This is a helpful tool if a photo is taken with too much or too little light.

Transparency: Make your photos semitransparent so you can overlap them and see through them by decreasing the opacity value. To make your image fully opaque, set the opacity to 100 percent.

Saturation: Intensify or decrease the colors of your image by increasing or lowering the saturation value. The lower the number, the less color in your photo. Zero percent saturation is grayscale.

Blur: Use this tool to remove sharp edges and detail from the image.

Grayscale: De-saturates photos to black, white, and shades of gray.

Project Details

DREAM DRESS
Once the photos were converted to grayscale, Traci was able to rely on them to tell the dress-shopping story. By choosing the one photo of Alison looking in a mirror as the largest on the page, we instantly know what this page is about. Traci then added smaller, related photos around the edge of the large photo. Because they overlapped a little bit, she added a thin white border to the smaller photos so they didn't blend into the large one. A short title and minimal journaling are used since the photos were intended to be the powerful focus of the page.

Dream
dress

It was one
of thoes fairy
tale moments
when Julie tried on her
wedding dress for the first
time. We knew it was the one.

pre-parties

The maid of honor often has a hand in all showers and bachelorette parties, so it's her job to save a clean invitation; a favor; and copies of poems, songs, or toasts for a scrapbook.

If you are planning a shower, make sure you designate one relative or bridesmaid to be the photographer. Ideally, this person has her own camera and enjoys taking photographs. "This should also be someone who knows everyone and is in the loop. So if there is a surprise guest or a sentimental gift from mom, she'll know to capture those key moments," says Anne. If this task usually falls on your shoulders, here are a few basic tips for problem-free photos:

HOW TO AVOID POINT AND "OH, SHOOT"

- **Get a new perspective.** Before snapping away, take a second to see if you have the best angle for your shot. If you are photographing kids or people sitting, consider kneeling to get on their level. If you're standing in front of a tall building, tilt the camera upward to get the whole shot.

- **Read the manual.** Your camera has many capabilities, from enhancing landscape shots to portraits and different modes for your flash. Take a minute to read through the camera's manual and take some experimental shots before the big day.

- **Keep shooting.** Take more than one photo of a moment. Not only does this increase your chances of getting a great shot, it might lend itself to a great scrapbook page of sequence shots.

- **To flash or not to flash.** That's a good question. Surprisingly, you may not need the flash indoors, and may need it outside. See if your camera has a "fill flash" to brighten up pictures taken in the shade. Experiment inside with other light sources and if you want something more dramatic, capture faces in the glow of candles or Christmas tree lights. Whatever you do, don't change the flash setting for a special shot and then forget to put it back to normal for the rest of the day!

- **Get ready for a close up.** Don't be afraid to try out your zoom or take a few giant steps toward your subject. A common mistake is to shoot from too far away and miss all the great facial expressions. You don't need to see everyone's shoes in all the pictures, so go ahead and get close.

- **Crop in your head.** Instead of relying on cropping photos once they are printed, compose the picture as you're taking it so you'll get the shot you want the first try.

- **Use portrait and landscape.** When shooting a person or a couple, rotate the camera to capture their length in a portrait shot, cropping them at their waist, knees, or floor in front of their feet. When shooting a group, keep the camera level for a landscape shot, cropping them at their shoulders, waists, or floor in front of their feet.

- **Be a fly on the wall.** Don't always wait to hear "cheese" before you snap. Take candid shots of people not always looking at the camera. Don't be afraid to shoot mid-toast or when someone is belly laughing. Often the best and most memorable shots on a page are the unplanned ones.

Project Details

BRIDAL SHOWER
Designer Traci Turchin created a palette and theme for this page through the simple pink and green pattern she chose for the bottom half. She made all photo borders, writing, and solid colors match colors found in the pattern and even used the same type of flower to embellish the top-right corner. Using elements of the same design throughout a page helps maintain continuity and avoid clutter, keeping the focus on the photos and words while presenting them with a stylish flair.

Bridal
Shower

the wedding day

A day as special as your wedding day deserves a professional photographer to document it. Whether you hire someone you found in a glossy bridal magazine or have assigned the duties to your camera-toting Uncle Bob, the most important thing for you to do is to think through the shots you want and communicate these expectations to your photographer.

Lisa Neighbors, owner of Blonde Tulip Wedding Photography in San Francisco, loves to photograph meaningful details of a wedding because she knows the couple has spent the last year thinking about them. "It's really important for me to know that the bride is wearing her great grandmother's earrings so we're positive I will get that shot," says Lisa.

Lisa's first piece of advice: Make a list of all the shots and people you are hoping to get. "It's such a hectic time that I literally go through with a pen and cross off each one when we get it," says Lisa. "This way we're sure we won't miss a grouping."

Lisa also suggests setting the stage for your photos. For her own wedding, Lisa opted not to get dressed at her parents' house because she knew it would be chaotic and not offer the clean, romantic background she had in mind for her photographs. Instead, she got ready in the bridal suite where she was married. "It's a matter of thinking of these details," says Lisa. "For example, I always bring a silk-padded hanger to shoot weddings because people spend thousands of dollars on their dress and have it hanging on a cheap plastic hanger."

A UNIQUE ALBUM

A professional photographer can offer a traditional wedding album. For something different, wedding expert Anne Chertoff shares some ideas for creating unique, original scrapbooks.

Meet in the middle. Starting from the front of a bound book, chronicle the bride's life from when she was a little girl and work your way to the center of the book, ending when she met her fiancé. Turn the book over and working from the back, add photos of the groom as a baby and gradually chart his life until he "meets" his future wife in the center of the book. Have their courting days and wedding as the center spread.

Cook up something good. Use blank cards and instructions instead of a guest book for guests to share something special with the bride. This can be a family recipe, advice for a good marriage, or simply good wishes. Collect the cards in a glass bowl and add them to an album with candid photos from the wedding.

Create your own "face book." Remember looking through the face book your first year at college? Now you can make your own as a fun way to help you and your future spouse get to know each other's friends and extended family. Make sure to get a photo of everyone at the wedding. Buy a blank address book and write in everyone's contact information and paste in their pictures.

Just
the
Girls

With this Ring

Project Details

JUST THE GIRLS (page 67)

This bride emphasized her desire for a photo of "just the girls" and was able to dedicate a page to her two nieces who served as her special flower girls. Designer Renée Foss created energy and movement by combining striped patterns with flowers, using a portrait mat under the landscape photo, and extending a ribbon horizontally to the few words on the tag attached to the page. The entire page is done in shades of lavender and green to coordinate with the photo, and the striped mat on the left was trimmed to a scalloped edge before being adhered to the page.

WITH THIS RING (opposite and below)

Sometimes, photos won't take center stage on a layout. To build excitement for a photo of one of the most significant moments of a wedding ceremony—when the rings are being exchanged—designer Lara Scott created a cover page adorned with a title and fleur-de-lis. For a dreamy, sophisticated style, Lara printed her title on to vellum paper then attached the cover with hinges so the photo could be hidden underneath. The page was then embellished with flowers to enhance the feeling of romance.

happily ever after

When Wendy Lundgren returned from her honeymoon, her husband immediately entrenched himself into renovating their new home. "Without a wedding to plan anymore and him having a project, I needed something to keep me busy, too," the teacher from Chicago says. She chose scrapbooking.

Though still high from her Hawaiian adventure, Wendy's first scrapbook project documented the transformation of their new house, which they completely gutted and rebuilt. She started out having fun, but the project was long and most of her photos were of furnaces and plumbing. She signed up for an out-of-town weekend retreat for inspiration only to realize when she arrived that she left all her materials for this project at home. Determined to be productive, Wendy purchased a wedding kit and switched gears.

Starting with her honeymoon, Wendy chose bright colors and beach themes and even aimed to use an album her new husband bought her from Hawaii. "I added snippets of things that we weren't likely to remember, like the name of a special drink from cocktail hour that was delicious but so strong we had to share it. Or how I had the best meal of my life on a dinner cruise and to this day I don't know what it was that I ate!"

Wendy may not be scrapping the events of her wedding in order, but she plans to add all the aspects of her engagement, her rehearsal dinner, and her bridal showers. However, she's left with what's commonly known to brides as a box of stuff. This box may include RSVP cards, a dried up boutonnière, napkins, ribbon, congratulatory cards, and the like. Like a lot of newlyweds, Wendy doesn't know what to do with this box, and can't bear to throw out its contents.

"This can be overwhelming," empathizes wedding expert Anne Chertoff. "You have a lot of great keepsakes but don't feel compelled to put every single item in a scrapbook." Choose the cards that are the most meaningful or the funniest, or simply have your grandmother's handwriting. If you don't want to throw away the rest, buy an archival box to store them in.

When archiving items, keep in mind that ticket stubs from your first date, maps from your honeymoon, and programs from your wedding may be printed on nonarchival quality paper. This doesn't mean you can't save these precious scraps, however. Your options:

Spray away. Visit your local craft store for de-acidification sprays that neutralize the acid contained in the paper.

Copy cat. Scan or photocopy your items onto acid-free paper. If you have a scanner, you can save the mementos as an image and import it right into the scrapbook software. This is a great solution for oversized or bulky items—even fabrics or flowers.

another day in *Paradise*

OUR
HONEYMOON

Hawaii

Separate but equal. Keep your potentially risky items on their own page or in a pocket, not directly touching a photo.

Wendy's scrapbook of her house is very different from her honeymoon album. Since the photos don't lend themselves too much journaling, she sticks mostly with titles. The one thing both albums do have in common is an abundance of photos.

PICS APLENTY

When you have a ton of photos you want to include on a layout, but still want a clean, attractive page, try one of these tips.

- **Flip out.** Add a mini album to the page that can accordion-fold out with more photos.

- **Pick a pocket.** Create a sleeve or an envelope to store stray photos.

- **Grid and bear it.** Tightly crop your photos then line them up edge to edge to make a collage.

- **Get framed.** Use smaller photos all cropped to the same size and from the same theme to frame a larger photo.

Project Details

HONEYMOON (page 71)

Designer Lara Scott was able to add extra honeymoon shots to this layout by creating an accordion book made out of tags. She attached the tags end to end, adhered photos to the inside of them, folded them front and back, and decorated the cover of the book with Hawaiian-themed images. For the display photos, she used the Mountaincow scrapbook software to manipulate them to the sizes she preferred. She added a transparency page with the title overlaying the sunset photo and gave the photos of the couple a scalloped edge to differentiate the two.

MEMENTOS (opposite)

This page captures the details of a wedding—the invitation, the flowers, and the place cards. Lara attached an actual copy of an invitation and the couple's place card, and used photos to set the scene of how the place cards were laid out to welcome the guests. She found a paper version of the flowers the bride carried down the aisle so they could easily be glued to the layout.

 See the Bonus CD for Make an Accordion Book how-to video.

MR. AND MRS.
STEVE BANTIN

MR. AND MRS.
JOHN BANDELL

MISS JAIME BLANC

MR. AND MR
JACK B

Emma

GEORGE AND LILY ANDERSON
REQUEST THE HONOR OF YOUR PRESENCE
AT THE MARRIAGE OF THEIR DAUGHTER
EMMA RENEE
TO
ANDREW EDWARD FOSTER
SUNDAY JUNE TWENTY-SIXTH
TWO THOUSAND AND FIVE
FOUR O'CLOCK IN THE AFTERNOON
RIVER BEND COUNTRY CLUB
ELMSRIDGE, NEW YORK

Andrew

EMMA AND ANDREW FOSTER
table 1

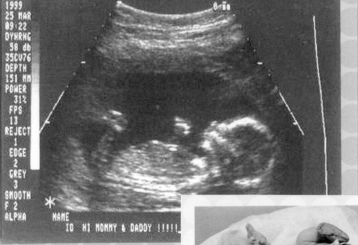

```
1999
25 MAR
09:22
DYNRNG
58 db
35CV76
DEPTH
151 MM
POWER
31%
FPS
13
REJECT
1
EDGE
2
GREY
3
SMOOTH
F 2
ALPHA
           NAME
           ID  HI MOMMY & DADDY !!!!!
```

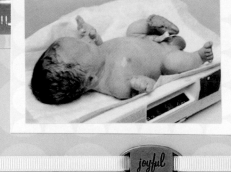

So many firsts. The first time we heard your heartbeat. The first time we saw you wriggling around on the ultrasound. The first time we held you.

joyful

Liz was gorgeous and gigant[ic] and such a trooper as sh[e] graciously smiled and hugge[d] each guest, played games an[d] opened gifts at he[r]

Baby Shower

firsts. The first
[w]e heard your
. The first time we
wriggling around
[ul]trasound. The first
[w]e held you.

chapter 5
for the baby

Tiny eyelashes. Rolls and rolls of thighs. Dimpled hands. These baby features may not last forever, but by creating meaningful layouts from your photos and keepsakes, you'll never forget them no matter how sleep deprived you get looking after them.

 pregnancy

When Rebecca Feld, a first grade teacher in Los Angeles, was pregnant with her son Harrison, a friend gave her a beautiful baby album with a gift certificate for a private scrapbook lesson.

Once she had her baby and loads of photos from her pregnancy and the hospital, she cashed in her gift. "It was like a crash course in cropping, and I couldn't stop!" says Rebecca. "As a teacher, I saw scrapbooking as making miniature bulletin boards, but this time I wasn't fighting with the paper. I was instantly hooked."

After finishing Harrison's baby book, she went back and created scrapbooks for her two older children.

"I start each album showing me pregnant. For my oldest, Katie, I have a picture of her daddy and me at our wedding, a page about who she's named after, and a page about the grandparents she never met," explains Rebecca.

The next series of shots are photos of her ultrasound. "I titled that page 'Under Construction' and designed it like a construction site with trucks and mounds of brown paper," she laughs.

THE FIRST PICTURES

Your sonogram is really the first photo of your baby, so it's only natural to want to add it to your scrapbook, just like any memento. However, unlike your acid-free paper and adhesives, hospital bracelets and brochures may be a risk to preserving your photos.

STAY FOCUSED

Since this page is dedicated to the first glimpses of the new baby both before and after birth, the spot on the page where your eye is drawn first—the focal point of the page—is the sonogram. In this case, the sonogram is larger than the other photo and is the only black-and-white item on the page, creating a striking contrast to the brightly saturated colors everywhere else.

Once you know what story your page is telling, the first step is to choose what to make your focal point. For example, if you want to document the day your baby is born (versus the actual birth), a photo of the grandparents eagerly sitting in the waiting room should be the focal point instead of the new baby itself.

Beyond using size and color to bring attention to a photo, you can mat it differently than the rest of the photos on the page, crop it into a unique shape, or adhere it on an angle if the rest of the photos are lined up straight.

KEEPING BALANCE

When looking at a layout, you're likely not to notice if it's balanced—you'll just like it. An unbalanced layout, however, will stand out to you because something on the page will be too small or large, an odd shape, or in the wrong place.

There are several reasons Traci's layout feels balanced. First, the journal box and the color photo of the baby combined have equal visual weight to the larger photo of the sonogram above them. Also, the baby, though in very different stages of his life, is in the same fetal position in both photos so there is a sense of symmetry and repetition, qualities that help balance a layout.

Project Details

FIRST GLIMPSES

Creating a focal point can be done in a number of ways. In this case, Traci relied on the sonogram's size and contrasting grayscale to draw attention to the photos. Having the ribbon run behind the journal box draws attention to the broken line and thus to what the page has to say in the journal text. The rest of the layout stuck strictly to the color palette of green, blue, and yellow, using lighter and darker shades of the same colors and smaller and larger circles in the same pattern to tie everything together and keep the eye focused on the photos.

```
1999
25 MAR
09:22
DYNRNG
58 db
35CV76
DEPTH
151 MM
POWER
  31%
FPS
  13
REJECT
  1
EDGE
  2
GREY
  3
SMOOTH
F 2
ALPHA    NAME
         ID  HI MOMMY & DADDY !!!!!
```

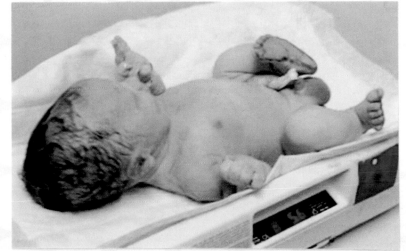

So many firsts. The first time we heard your heartbeat. The first time we saw you wriggling around on the ultrasound. The first time we held you.

joyful

getting ready

"Where's the book when you're pregnant with me?" asks Ashley Morick, age five. What started out as a scrapbook her mom, Amy, made to document her pregnancy, has since turned into a favorite bedtime story.

"I kept a pregnancy journal for both of my children," says Amy. "I have all my sonograms and photos of me pregnant and I kept track of all the facts. What we did to celebrate finding out we were having a baby, how much I weighed, what I couldn't eat. My kids get a kick out of that."

As for Amy's baby shower, Ashley was lucky enough to attend. "We had a shower after she was born, so all the cards I received were extra special since they were all welcoming her," says Amy. "So I have one scrapbook dedicated to all the keepsakes from the shower. Since then, I've added cards from her first Christmas, first birthday, and other holidays."

RULE OF THIRDS

Once you have your photos and important memories gathered, you may not know where to start. One trick is to imagine your page has lines dividing it into thirds both horizontally and vertically. The points where these lines cross, the inside corners of nine squares, are spots on a page the eye is instinctively drawn to. Therefore, they are a good starting place for placing the photos or embellishments you want to have the most attention.

ZEE PAGE LAYOUT

Another trick to laying out a page is to place your items in a letter Z formation. Since this is how we instinctively read a book or sign, the eye will naturally start at the top left and follow the path of a Z across the design, down diagonally, and then across again to the bottom right.

ALPHABET SOUP

If you are planning a baby shower, assign each guest a letter of the alphabet and instruct her to send you a photo that features something cute for the baby that begins with that letter. Then scrap a page around each photo and its letter to create baby's first ABC book and present it to the expectant mom at the shower.

Project Details

BABY SHOWER

Traci arranged the photos, flowers, and journal in a Z layout allowing the eye to move back and forth to each picture. The main photo gets right to the "point" of the page by showing her friend pointing right at Justine's pregnant belly. The yellow flowers play up the bright accent color also used for the vertical stripe down the page and the journaling.

Liz was gorgeous and gigantic and such a trooper as she graciously smiled and hugged each guest, played games and opened gifts at her

Baby Shower

the baby's here!

You've prepared nine months—if not longer!—for this moment. Now the baby is here and you want to document every significant moment of his or her life. Nick Kelsh, an Olympus visionary photographer and author of *How to Photograph Your Baby*, can help translate these important moments into beautiful scrapbook pages.

"I really do believe you can express your love with a camera," says Nick. "The ability to always have a close-up picture of someone you love is really straight from the heart."

Nick's operative words are "close up." Of his three cardinal photo-taking rules, getting close to your subject is number one. "So often you see a photo of this little tiny person in the center of a big frame with lots of space around them. You simply need to get closer to your subject," advises Nick.

For a dramatic scrapbook page, Nick suggests always including a close-up. "I've seen layouts where every person in every picture is full length and the eye doesn't know where to go," warns Nick. Give your pages "visual variety" by including a landscape photo with photos of a person from the waist up with the full-length shots.

Nick also subscribes to the philosophy that less can be more. "Sometimes, one little picture on a page is a beautiful thing. It makes it a little gem."

VISUAL TRIANGLE

Placing elements onto a page in a triangle helps the eye travel from one image to the next. In this page, Traci balanced the close up of the baby with the photos of the parents. If you were to draw a line from the baby's face to each of the parent's, or if you were to connect all the brown accents on the page, you'd see the triangles.

SYMMETRY

An easy way to create balance on a page is to make one side of the page symmetrical to the other. In this case, Renée balanced the right side of the page with a photo of the same size on the left side of the page. The harlequin pattern blocks and the striped lines are also of equal weight and mirrored across the page. Similarly, one photo is captioned at the top, and the other photo is captioned at the bottom.

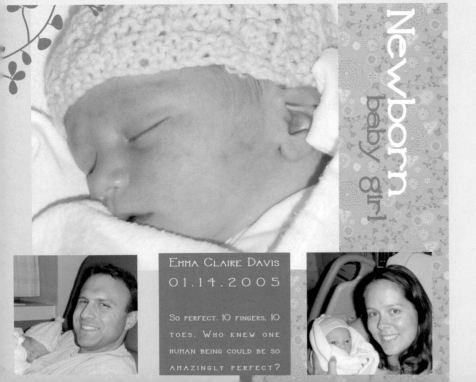

Newborn baby girl

EMMA CLAIRE DAVIS
01.14.2005

SO PERFECT. 10 FINGERS. 10 TOES. WHO KNEW ONE HUMAN BEING COULD BE SO AMAZINGLY PERFECT?

Newborn
baby boy

COLE NATHAN DAVIS
01.14.2005

So perfect. 10 fingers, 10 toes. Who knew one human being could be so amazingly perfect?

THREE WAYS TO GET BETTER PHOTOS OF YOUR BABY:

1. **Get closer.** "Ask yourself what you want in this photo and fill the frame with it," says Nick.

2. **Go click crazy.** The more photos you take, the more likely you'll get a great one. "You increase your luck factor."

3. **Experiment with your flash off.** "Your camera's flash is essentially like the headlights from your car," explains Nick. The bright, unnatural light destroys any mood lighting. However, sometimes you have no choice if there is no alternative light source. Determining this will take some experimentation and time.

Project Details

IT'S A BOY (page 81)

The large, central close-up of the baby's face causes the eye to linger and visually appreciate the beauty of the sleeping baby. By adding the parents' photos to the bottom right and left, Traci forms a triangle that visually ties the baby into context with love and family. The central journal, announcing baby Cole, is highlighted by using white text on a darker brown background. The chrysanthemum pattern and the callout graphic of the branch at the top left emphasize the delicate, peaceful nature of the subject. A balanced scrapbook layout, like a carefully crafted poem, can be used to accentuate the mood and meaning present but easily missed when viewing the photos alone.

Using your computer to scrapbook enables you to quickly adapt existing layouts to new subjects. This layout is easily transformed for a girl baby by changing the blue pattern to pink and changing the photos to grayscale.

BABY FACE (opposite)

The repeated and overlapping symmetry of the layout lets the eye spend most of its time appreciating the two photos. Desaturating the photos to grayscale further brings them to the front of our attention, standing out among the calm, orderly arrangement of elements and the soft pastel colors. The single item of asymmetry finally draws our eye to the framed monogram once we are done appreciating the photos.

SWEET *child of mine*

SIMPLY *adorable*

HRF

▢ firsts

Rachel Schleich has a file on her computer titled "Milestones." Since her daughter Christiana was born, Rachel has kept a log of all her baby's firsts and the date they happened. "When I went back to scrapbook her first year, all her milestones were in one place. I had written down certain songs that she loved," says Rachel. "It takes two seconds for me to type something quickly. I don't even use full sentences, just enough to remember."

LAST, BUT NOT LEAST

Don't fret, however, if you don't have a recollection of the first time your baby sneezed or rolled over. Inevitably, no matter how much younger siblings are loved, they are simply not as well documented as the firstborn. Photographer Nick Kelsh has a solution. "I don't take tons of photographs of my kids, I just try to take really nice ones. Every year I have about six or ten really great photographs. So if by the time your child is ten years old you have 100 beautiful photographs, I think that's better than 500 mediocre ones," says Nick.

To get those really good ones, Nick suggests having a photo session. Ideally, find time when you're alone with your subject so you can concentrate without distractions. Then take a roll of film of your child by a window to get what Nick calls "soft side lighting."

STOP COPYING ME

Emma's reaction to tasting peas for the first time turned into an impromptu photo shoot.

Renée created a completely asymmetrical layout where no one side is a mirror image of the other. It remains balanced, however, because the embellishments, patterns, and words take up as much visual space as the two off-centered photos. Asymmetry can be used effectively as long as the visual weight of the images used is balanced.

PLAY IT AGAIN, SAM

Just like a song might repeat a chorus to create a rhythm, a layout can utilize repetition for the same effect. Repeat photos, shapes, and sizes and your page will have a unified design. Repeating a picture, a color, or a shape will reinforce a theme, whether it's a first smile or school spirit. Two photos of Emma's first pea experience were used to reinforce the theme of the page.

❋ See the Bonus CD for Make a Layout in 3 Minutes how-to video.

Project Details

FIRST PEAS

If you have tranquil photos of your sweet baby sleeping, keep the layout just as serene. But if the moment you're scrapbooking was a pandemonium of pureed peas and belly laughs, don't be afraid to reflect that in your layout too. Renée's use of patterns and embellishments didn't detract from Emma's photos but created movement and energy.

Emma

first Peas

Emma's first experience with peas did not go very well! She really liked cereal by that point, so she was willing to accept the spoon into her mouth. Until she got her first taste of the peas, that is!

e

B O Y

Cole didn't quite know what to make of his first birthday party! Why were all of these

happy 1st birthday

Cole really enjoyed when everyone sang Happy Birthday to him. He wanted it again and again! But then he tried to grab his candle and didn't understand why everyone started yelling. The only thing that stopped his tears was his first birthday cake!

FIRST BIRTHDAY. SUCH A BIG

BOY

Cole didn't quite know what to make of his first birthday party! Why were all of these people here at once? Why did mommy keep strapping this paper cone thing on my head? What's this yummy squishy stuff and when can I have some more?

Cole

COLE EATS CAKE

chapter 6

for the birthday boy or girl

Everybody gets to celebrate a birthday one day each year, so it makes sense we can't get enough of birthday scrapbook ideas. We love celebrating our own birthdays, our kids' birthdays, our family members' birthdays, and our friends' birthdays. All birthday details are significant: the age, the traditions, and the guests who help us celebrate them. Using embellishments can help tell a meaningful story for birthday boys and girls of all ages.

baby's first

"The wonderful thing about having a kid is you see the whole world completely new again. There are things as an adult you stop noticing," says Kim Hammer, owner of Bitty Cakes in North Carolina. "The other day Max noticed the trees didn't have leaves on them. He's starting to figure out seasons, which I just take for granted."

Birthdays are no different. Since Max's first birthday, Kim has renewed her love of the celebration. "Everyone is taking his picture, singing to him, and making a fuss. Now I remember why I loved birthdays as a child and I just get so excited for him," she says.

ALL THE FUSS

First birthday parties are an exciting milestone filled with gifts, photo-taking, frosting, family, and sometimes a bunch of other one-year-olds. "If this page seems chaotic, it's because what's happening in the photos was chaotic," says designer Renée Foss of her "Such a Big Boy!" layout. "The layout is busier than I typically do, but I had fun with it because the page needed to be more energetic to convey all the activity in the photos."

Renée used a number of different embellishments to create this energy. However, she kept her photos the main focus. Her general rule for using embellishments: she uses one large embellishment and one small one; it's a matter of trial and error—laying out all your potential flourishes when you start—and playing around with them until you find the right combination and placement.

HEAVY METAL

Having two boys, Renée finds she uses a lot of metal embellishments because they have a masculine flair. "I always joke that I could never bring my scrapbooks on an airplane because I would never get through the metal detector!" she laughs. In addition to working well with her boyish layouts, metal embellishments, such as brads and photo anchors, are a popular choice because they are also functional. This decorative hardware can also attach pages together, hold a photo in place, grasp a ribbon—all while adding dimension and design. "I don't use a lot of glitter or rhinestones, so I look to metal for that added sheen," says Renée.

LESS IS MORE

Before the big day, Kim taught Max how to blow out the candles but when the moment came, he wasn't following the program. Instead, he lifted his arm to smack out the candle. "These photos are like movie stills to tell the whole story of that moment," Kim says. "You can see him excited about the cake, making the blow face, and then lifting his arm, and my reactions." Because the sequence of the photos on this page is so important, designer Traci Turchin decided to

forgo any additional flourishes to the "Happy First Birthday" layout on page 91. Remember, embellishments are made to enhance a page design not detract from it.

START OF SOMETHING GOOD

Consider creating a scrapbook just for birthdays. Buy a scrapbook and add your child's first birthday layout as your inaugural spread. Create a label for the spine of the book so you can easily identify it for each year and decorate the cover with a photo of your child or a birthday theme. You can also add the party's invitation, the guest list, and even highlight significant presents.

FIRST BIRTHDAY

SUCH A BIG

BOY

Cole didn't quite know what to make of his first birthday party! Why were all of these people here at once? Why did mommy keep strapping this paper cone thing on my head? What's this yummy squishy cake stuff and when can I have some more?

Cole

COLE EATS CAKE

yummy, yummy, yummy

Cole

FEELING OVERWHELMED IN THE EMBELLISHMENTS AISLE? READ ON...

Beads: Add beads to a page by threading them on embroidery floss or craft wire, or pour micro beads onto glue for subtle shimmer.

Brads: You might remember brads—also called paper fasteners—from the days of learning how to tell time. A brad is what held the two hands of the clock to the construction paper so you could move them to different hours. A brad is traditionally a brass dome with two prongs that slip through the page and then split on the backside to hold in place. Now brads come in an endless variety of sizes, shapes, and colors.

Buttons: A whimsical and readily available item, a button can be attached by literally sewing it onto the page or by just using a strong glue dot.

Eyelets: You may not realize this, but you've been using eyelets your whole life. They're those circular holes on your sneakers that your laces go through. On a scrapbook page, however, they can have a lot of uses. They can attach pages together, hang charms, thread ribbon, or simply be decorative. Eyelets need specific tools to be set. Check your craft store for a kit including a punch, setter, hammer, and mat.

Fabric and lace: Small pieces go a long way. Check sale bins and discontinued sample books.

Flowers: Dried flowers can add a delicate, romantic notion to a spread. Attach carefully using a spray adhesive

Hinges: A creative way to hide photos of personal journals, hinges are usually attached with eyelets.

Ribbons and fibers: A no-fail, affordable way to add borders to photos, ribbon and fibers can be laced through eyelets, tied in bows and knots, and used to attach pieces together.

Stickers: Stickers can do more than just, well, stick. Add dimension by making them unsticky with powder and then attaching with foam tape. Or find mirror-image stickers and marry half of them together and attach the other sides to the page for a three-dimensional effect.

Studs, nailheads, and conchos: These all fall into a category of embellishments that attach to the page with tiny, sharp prongs. These prongs are poked through a page that is lying on some sort of padding such as a mousepad or cardboard. Once inserted, turn the page over and bend each prong back with a wooden stick or the back of an old spoon.

Tags and die cuts: There is no end to the variety of shapes, sizes, colors, and themes of die cuts. They can be used as journal boxes, frames, or simply decorative flair.

Wire: Thin craft wire can be a beautiful, though ambitious, addition to a scrapbook page. You can thread it with beads or bend it into a word or flowers.

STICKY FINGERS

Many types of adhesive are available depending on the weight of your embellishment. Consider choosing an acid-free product to ensure the longevity of your scrapbook.

Double-sided tape: An easy way to adhere multiple layers of paper or other flat materials, double-sided tape is affordable and available in a variety of dispensers.

Foam tape: Similar to double-sided tape but with a layer of foam in between the layers of adhesive, foam tape is used to raise a layer of cardstock or a photo above the rest of the layout, creating extra height for a more three-dimensional design when embellishing with paper.

Glue dots: Available in craft stores, glue dots come in different sizes and are one of the stickiest choices for heavier embellishments such as metal tags or rhinestones. They don't fasten immediately, allowing you to reposition, but once set there is no getting them off.

Glue Pen: Best for applying glue to small embellishments or in hard-to-reach places.

Hot glue gun: There are more scrapbook-friendly options for a strong adhesive, such as glue dots, than this potentially dangerous option, though glue guns are ideal for heavy duty crafts.

Paste: A staple of any kindergarten class, paste, glue sticks, and good old Elmer's glue can always do in a pinch, especially when scrapbooking with children. Best for working with paper.

Photo tabs: Easy to fasten to pictures with no risk of harming photos.

Photomount spray: Perfect for lightweight or delicate embellishments such as flower petals or sand.

Removable tape: This tape is designed to be temporary so you can reposition or remove it at any time. Perfect for holding stencils in place.

Transparent tape: There are many varieties of tape that hide their presence, including vellum tape for taping vellum envelopes invisibly, and transparent tape for sealing the edges of a page, taping something closed, or taping along the outside of a layer.

Xyron machine: Enables any small embellishment to get a layer of self-adhesive and become a sticker.

❀ See All About Adhesives how-to video on the Bonus CD.

Project Details

SUCH A BIG BOY! (page 89)

Use embellishments to help tell the story in the layout. In this case, Renée added words to her tags and photo anchors as captions for her photos. She captures the chaos of the day by matching it with a busy, hectic layout and strong colors. She uses multiple, smaller photos to walk the viewer through the busy action and avoid highlighting any one single moment.

HAPPY FIRST BIRTHDAY (below)

Traci treated the "1st" in the title as an embellishment by having it stand out as an accent color on the page. This could be printed as part of the background or printed separately, cut out, and adhered to the page with foam tape to raise it above the page. Again, a sequence of photos is used to capture and animate the memory of the silliness and unpredictability that a baby can bring into life.

Cole really enjoyed when everyone sang Happy Birthday to him. He wanted it again and again! But then he tried to grab his candle and didn't understand why everyone started yelling. The only thing that stopped his tears was his first birthday c a k e !

 license to party

The birthdays that mark the end of the terrible twos, the start of being a teenager, or the legal right to drive are life landmarks. Create a scrapbook page to capture the metamorphosis of growing up.

ALL FUN AND GAMES

For a party full of little ones, snap photos of all the party games and when it's time to open the presents, try getting a close-up shot of each child and their gift along with the birthday boy or girl. This is a great way to really document who was at the party—something that will be cherished one day when the whole class isn't being invited to parties anymore.

These photos can also serve double duty. When making prints for your scrapbook, print a double and send it with a thank-you note.

This will teach your child a great habit to get into, and the guest will enjoy seeing the important role he played in your child's party.

SIMPLY CONSISTENT

A simple embellishment, such as a single ribbon, is a great element to bring from page to page to unify an entire birthday scrapbook. Also consider adding continuity year after year by always taking a birds-eye photo of the birthday cake and cutting away the background to turn it into a die-cut style embellishment.

Project Details

KELLY'S BIRTHDAY PARTY

Borders play a significant role in this layout. They serve as frames for all the photos and the one large journaling block. Traci highlighted three detail shots at the bottom of the page and layered a translucent "17" on the center one to add more information about the birthday celebration. She also layered her title behind her journal for added dimension. The delicate ribbon embellishments at the corners give the page a clean, uncluttered, and feminine element of three dimensionality.

traditions

"By nine in the morning, every single one of my in-laws had called me, didn't say hello but just launched into the birthday song," laughs Ken Cornick, who recently joined a family of birthday enthusiasts from New Jersey.

"I've never seen a family get so excited about birthdays. Not just their own, but everyone else's too!"

Ken quickly got used to the birthday attention and looks forward to walking into his children's room on their birthday morning, waking them up with singing and presents.

Every family has their own thing—always ordering chocolate soufflé, marking a new height on a kitchen wall, taking a photo standing in front of dad to see how much the birthday boy or girl has grown over the year.

THE START OF SOMETHING

For Sabrina Eisen's third birthday, her parents filled their dining room with balloons for what they thought was just festive decor. They didn't realize that by the next birthday, Sabrina would insist on a balloon-filled room. After that, balloons were synonymous with birthdays for both children.

Project Details

BALLOON ROOM (pages 94–95)

Designer Traci Turchin could have opted for balloon-shaped stickers or some balloon clip art to embellish a page about balloons. Instead, she used four small delicate flowers to fill the white space above the title. Because the photos really captured the essence of the balloons, Traci felt balloon embellishments would compete with the photos and take the layout over the top.

When choosing embellishments, don't feel compelled to find stickers or trinkets to exactly match your theme. Instead, go with what feels right and simply looks pretty.

My "baby" sister is not so much a baby anymore! Her birthday party had all the traditional birthday fixin's...cupcakes (confetti batter and frosting--Kelly's favorite), family, balloons, streamers...and a girl one year older and wiser. It's impossible not to be proud of the person Kelly is. Generous, hilarious, fun, loving, and quite the budding scientist! I always look forward to coming home and visiting her on the weekends and catching up with all of her latest adventures! She's ready to tackle her senior year of high school and I can't wait to see how she grows this year!   1 June 2003.

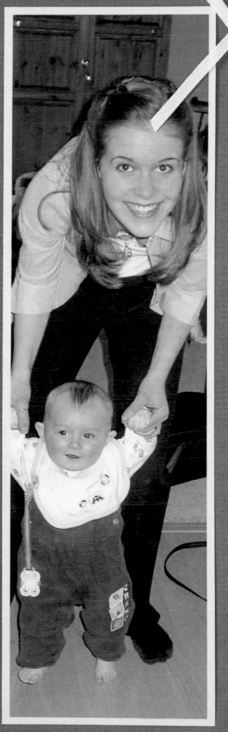

17 years old

balloon room

Jake's second birthday

Jake's third birthday

Anna's fourth birthday

oons, but in our family we take it to a love
next level! For each birthday we fill the
alloons. Jake and Anna love to pick their
will spend their entire birthday month
o colors to pick! How did this balloon
e so many good traditions, it began as an
up dozens of balloons in preparation for
y party and planned to string them up
ather had other ideas. It was so windy and
ed our balloon inside, and then decided
e balloon fest! Blowing up dozens of
y (nor is cleaning them up), but keeping
alive makes it all worth while!

traditions

Anna's sixth birthday

a milestone age

Krista Mettler is the self-appointed historian of her family. If any of her relatives find interesting photos in their attic, they're always sent directly to Krista because she'll turn them into wonderful collages of her family's significant events. A die-hard digital scrapbooker, Krista doesn't worry when every member of her family then wants a copy of her lay-outs. "I love that with digital layouts I can make prints for my aunt, cousin, and brother. I can make as many copies as I want and these photos aren't sitting in a box in a basement somewhere," she says.

Krista finds many more advantages to being a digital scrapbooker, especially the versatility of digital embellishments or "elements." "First of all, I love that my scrapbooks aren't five million inches thick," says Krista. "I can still add depth and layers, I just do that with drop shadows now."

TRADITIONAL VS. DIGITAL

The benefit of using Mountaincow's scrapbooking software is you never have to decide which team you're on; you can dabble in both digital and traditional scrapbooking and get the best of both worlds.

Recolor. Match digital ribbon to the exact color green of the shirt your son is wearing in the photo you want to frame.

Redo. That font not what you had in mind? The ribbon too thick? Just click and erase. You can tweak a layout until you think it's absolutely perfect.

Reuse. All digital elements, photos, and patterns can be used over and over again.

WE GOT CUT OFF

Designer Traci Turchin used one large digital flower to embellish a page about Nana's eightieth birthday. The two-dimensional flower is a perfect contrast to the group shot of the entire family. The flower is given a fun twist by being cropped by the edge of the page, a technique easily done in a digital layout.

INVOLVE THE WHOLE FAMILY

As a matriarch or patriarch of a family reaches a monumental age, you can be sure to include all facets of that person's life into a scrapbook by involving the whole family. With the right planning, you can have a gift the guest of honor will absolutely treasure.

Before the party, put a package together for everyone on the guest list with the following items:

- Paper with the guest's name as a title on the top

- 4" x 6" (10.7 x 15.2 cm) photo frames

- Pen

- Acid-free adhesive strips

- Return envelope

Include clear instructions for the younger family members to create a page with a story and photo of themselves and the grand dame or master of the family. Give them a realistic due date so they can return the pages in time for you to bind them and give as a gift.

Project Details

NANA IS EIGHTY

Because the whole family came to celebrate Nana's birthday, it was very important to have a large group shot on this page. Traci added only one single shot of the birthday girl with her cake and a simple flower to keep the layout as tasteful and sweet as the eightieth birthday party itself.

The entire family tourned out to wish Nana a Happy 80th birthday!

Nana is 80

Fifty years
married to my best friend

1954

2004

1985 · 2005 · 1985 · 2005 · 1985 · 2005
20 years

High School
Reunion 1985 2005

Brett and I had a great time going to our 20th high school reunion. I was thrilled to see my best friends Donna and Natalie and we had a blast reminiscing. I hope we don't wait another twenty years to do this again.

1954

2005 · 1985 · 2005 · 1985
20 years

chapter 7

celebrations

Precious photos of special occasions and milestone events can speak volumes about your life's journey. Baptisms, communions, bar and bat mitzvahs, graduations, proms, anniversaries, and reunions all stand out and help us mark our passage into adulthood and beyond. Help tell your story and enhance your memories with the right color palette to document these rites of passages for future generations to enjoy.

a golden anniversary...with hints of azure

Choosing colors for your scrapbook page is a huge task. For inspiration, it's best to turn to the photos you plan to use. Decide if you want to highlight a color used in the photo or if you'd rather find a color that will coordinate with the photo's background.

Once you've chosen your main color, you can choose the rest of the palette based on how other colors are related to the first color on the color wheel. A color wheel is basically a chart of the spectrum of colors. Technically, it's made of twelve primary, secondary, and tertiary hues and their tints and shades.

Color, while a pretty basic concept, has a lexicon of its own:

Primary colors: colors that can't be made by combining other colors. They are red, yellow, and blue.

Secondary colors: colors made from combining primary colors. They are orange, green, and purple.

Tertiary colors: colors made from combining primary and secondary colors, such as coral or aqua.

Tint: the color that results when white is added to a color.

Shade: the color that results when black is added to a color.

Tone: the color that results when gray is added to a color.

When you choose "More Colors" from the colors menu in the Mountaincow scrapbook software, you're looking at the color wheel in chart form.

EASY AS ONE-TWO-THREE
Three is the magic number of colors to use on one layout. Decide on a main color to use on the majority of the page (such as the background), choose a second color for accents (such as a journal box, title, or photo frames), and select a third color for accents, embellishments, a single word of the title, or a single photo mat.

In this anniversary layout, designer Traci Turchin started with blue as her main color, picked up from the sweater worn in the large photo and from the background of the original wedding photo. She chose a complementary color of yellow for the title, text, and flower for the bottom corner of the page. The green is a small accent color used to add a hint of contrast to the palette.

THANKS FOR THE COMPLEMENT
Complementary colors provide the most contrast of any other combinations, so use them when you really want a bold layout or want colors to "pop." This can work even with mute colors because you're creating energy from the relationship between the colors.

Project Details

FIFTY YEARS
For a "through the years" type of layout, it's always important to label your photos with dates for future generations. This layout would work as the cover page to an entire album made of the couple's fifty years as husband and wife since it contrasts an original wedding photo with a current photo of the couple fifty years later.

Fifty years

married to my best friend

1954

2004

reunion

One of Dayspring Fowler's most important scrapbook projects is an album dedicated to her husband, Ryan, and his service in the Navy. Dayspring started the book with Ryan's original statement when he applied to join the Navy, plus photos from his swearing in and graduation.

She's kept the colors very consistent for this album—you guessed it—in the Navy blue family with silver accents.

MONOCHROMATIC IS NOT MONOTONOUS

Choosing one color and using several of its shades in a layout is a no-fail plan for a beautiful page. You never have to worry about colors overpowering each other or clashing. Instead, you can create beautiful backgrounds to showcase your photos.

Monochromatic pages are also a great way to create serene and tranquil pages, perfect for photos of sunsets or sleeping children.

Project Details

HIGH SCHOOL REUNION

Designer Ursula Page safely stuck with shades of pink to create a summertime high school reunion layout. Starting with a paisley pattern, she picked up lighter and darker pinks in the title and the ribbon she chose to embellish the page.

COLOR SCHEMES

Once you have located the main color you are working with on a color wheel, you can look at the relationship other colors have to it to find your palette.

Analogous: Uses three consecutive colors on a wheel

Complementary: Uses direct opposite colors on the wheel

Split Complementary: Uses a color and the two colors on either side of its complement

Monochromatic: Uses a combination of tints and shades of one color

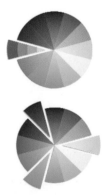

Triad: Uses three colors equidistant from one another on the color wheel

High School
Reunion 1985 2005

Brett and I had a great time going to our 20th high school reunion. I was thrilled to see my best friends Donna and Natalie and we had a blast reminiscing. I hope we don't wait another twenty years to do this again.

. 2005 . 1985 .
. 1985 . 2005 .
20 years

have faith

Inspired by a book she read when she was pregnant, Rebecca Dohndt held a blessing ceremony for each one of her three children and asked each of her relatives and close friends to bring a bead to create a spirit necklace. She tape-recorded the ceremony so she could later transcribe each blessing for a scrapbook page.

"I was amazed at how our families really embraced the ceremony," says Rebecca, a Philadelphia mom. "My in-laws made a bead from a tree in their yard in Utah, so a little piece of them would be part of this necklace."

In addition to photographs of all the friends and relatives who attended, Rebecca included the blessings she typed up plus the ones that were sent and emailed from those who couldn't make it. "I made sure it was all in the order of the beads so my child can see who each one is from and what it means."

TOO MANY CROSSES TO BEAR

Heidi Petereson, co-owner of Faith, Memories N' Stitches, a scrapbooking store in Vermont specializing in religious-themed supplies, is often asked to make communion and baptism pages.

Heidi's first step is to choose paper to go with her photos. "If you have a photo of a little girl in a bright pink dress, don't choose bright pink to mat your photo. This will only draw attention to her dress, rather than to your little girl," says Peterson. "Instead, chose a color that you want to bring out, such as the blue in her eyes."

Bringing your photos to your scrapbook store is always a great way to choose your paper and embellishments. Heidi's done plenty of impulse buying and has ended up with stickers or ribbon that don't fit on the page. "Sometimes there are things you just can't resist!" says Heidi.

What to do if you end up with extra doodads? Heidi recommends keeping them organized. This way, if you are scrapping with friends and they have a use for them, you can easily find them and swap for something you like that they have but don't need.

WHITE OUT

Designer Traci Turchin wanted to use a large amount of white space for this first communion layout to represent the purity of the occasion. She chose a light tint of blue patterned paper to coordinate with the deeper blue blazer being worn in the photos.

COLOR ME FOCUSED

For a layout of a bat mitzvah celebration, Traci chose a photo of the bat mitzvah girl standing with the Torah as the focal point to emphasize the purpose of the page. She chose the main page color—a soft lavender—to coordinate with the Torah cover and draw attention to the religious significance of the Torah for the event.

"I accented the page with blue because it's an analogous color to the purple and that's an easy way to create a pleasing color combination," explains Traci. A contrasting or complementary color would have been loud or stark. "The blue makes the purple softer and not so attention-grabbing."

communion

may 1979

COLOR MEANING

Want the colors you chose for your layout to have meaning? Consider the connotations of these colors.

Color	Meaning
Red	Powerful, hot
Burgundy	Rich
Pink	Romantic
Orange	Warm, earthy, friendly
Yellow	Exciting
Green	Fresh
Blue	Calm, cool
Purple	Royal
Lavender	Nostalgic
White	Pure

Project Details

COMMUNION (page 105)

The photos used in this layout had been stored in magnetic photo pages since they were taken in 1979. Since they had yellowed a bit, Traci scanned them into her computer to preserve and enhance them. In one photo, she was able to crop out the photographer's thumb that snuck into the frame. In another, she zeroed in on the subject by cropping out his classmates.

Traci created a simple, modular page to contrast with the late '70s style of the photos. "When working with dated photos, I prefer to go with a very classic design so that nothing clashes," says Traci. "If this were a photo from the '70s of a mini dress and mod hairdo and not of a religious milestone, I might have gone all out with a groovy bubble font." Instead, Traci stayed subdued so the pictures could stand on their own.

The original photos can now be preserved in an archive-safe place while copies of the photos are on display.

BAT MITZVAH (opposite)

Traci wanted to include all the special symbols and traditions of a bat mitzvah. Since this required using a lot of photos in the layout, she closely cropped the photos and lined them up edge to edge. Traci kept the page perfectly symmetrical—one large photo in the top left and bottom right corners and three smaller photos across from them—to keep it balanced.

✳ For a how-to video on color relationships, see the Bonus CD for Colors of Spring.

Maddie's
Bat Mitzvah

Temple Shalom
23 January 2004

school daze

Artist Jessica Clark, owner of iLand Art Gallery in Fenwick Island, Delaware, chronicled her high school years with photos of her on the cheerleading squad, newspaper clippings from big football games, and, of course, her best friends.

"It's hilarious to look at my high school scrapbooks now," she laughs. "High school is a really big changing point in everyone's life, physically and emotionally. Even from your freshman year to your senior year you can go from skinny girl with braces to growing into who you are now. Not every one has a bat mitzvah or goes to college, but almost everyone can relate to events from high school."

Jessica remembers stocking up when the yearbook committee had a sale of the photos they didn't use. "This gave me a chance to get beautiful black-and-white photos of guys I had crushes on that I wouldn't have had the guts to take myself!"

The scrapbooks Jessica makes today include a lot more of her own drawings and artwork, but if she had to do her high school albums over, she wouldn't change much. This way, she's still able to look at the books from a teenager's perspective.

GO TEAM
The only change Jessica would make to her albums now is incorporating more school spirit by adding school colors and the mascot.

Green and gold, in addition to being analogous colors, were appropriately used for the high school graduation layout to carryout the school colors. Because green was a predominant color in the photos, a lighter tint of green was used to keep the focus on the pictures.

PROM-ISE TO REMEMBER
Christina Capozzi wanted her prom pictures to show just how fabulous she and her friends looked all dressed up. In addition to using a really good camera, she developed the photos as 5" x 7" (12.7 x 17.8 cm) instead of the standard 4" x 6" (10.7 x 15.2 cm) size.

"I loved all the dresses and I thought having larger photos would be a great way to look back and see all the effort we put in our appearance," says Christina, now a junior at Ithaca College in New York.

Another way Christina made her prom scrapbook special is she made sure to name everyone in the photos in her journaling. "There's a chance I won't keep in touch with all my classmates, so this way I won't forget anyone's name."

Christina used an oversized album and placed all the photos in chronological order: photos at home with her family, one with her date, ones with her friends in the trolley they rented to get to the prom, and then tons of pictures of them dancing and the crowning ceremony.

"I just did a little doodling on the sides instead of using any stickers," explains Christina. "I didn't want anything to take away from the photos. Everyone's dresses made the photos very colorful and there was a lot of movement from all the goofy stuff we were doing. So I just accented with a gold pen since that was the color of my dress."

Graduation 2005

COMPUTER COLOR PICKER

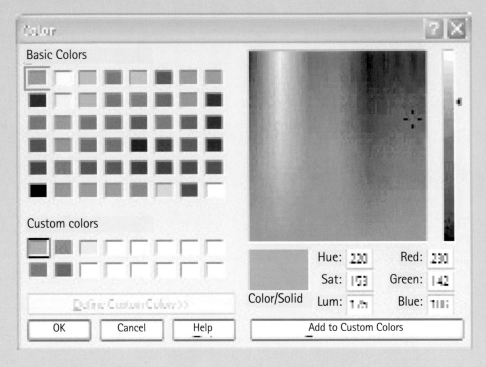

STRIKE A POSE

Add some variety and color to those uncomfortable, posed photos. Use the computer to crop and duplicate the photos several times, then recolor each photo a different primary or secondary color, Warhol-style.

When choosing a color with your computer's color picker, all the colors of the rainbow are spread out from left to right. These are the hues you can choose from. The saturation of the color is distributed from top to bottom, as all the colors on the bottom turn to gray. The slider on the right indicates the brightness of the color.

TETRAD'S A CHARM

The four colors chosen to recolor the photo are all equidistant from one another on the color wheel, creating a tetrad layout. For added dimension, a light blue-on-blue harlequin pattern is used as a background for most of the page, and a dark blue-on-blue harlequin pattern was used to mat the recolored photos.

Project Details

GRADUATION (page 109)

Cap and gown photos are essential when documenting a graduation. In this layout, all the necessary photos are included: a group shot of the entire graduating class, the graduate in line to accept his diploma, and close-ups of best friends.

PROM

Close-ups, school pictures, and baby mug shots all work well with the repeat and recolor technique. When using darker colors, adjust the brightness to lighten the photo so the image is still clear. Cropping the photo to a square before duplicating and recoloring gives you more options when laying out the repeated photos.

Prom
2005

Cooling **Off**

You may not be able to say the word "sprinkler", but you know how to stay cool on a hot summer day. Who knew a hose could be so fun?

You may not be able to say the word "sprinkler", but you know how to stay cool on a hot summer day. Who knew a hose could be so fun?

chapter 8

tips and techniques

turn your hobby into a business

Do your friends "ooh" and "aah" over your layouts and ask "How did you do that?" Do you make a lot of scrap-books as gifts? Has anyone ever asked you to scrapbook her photos? This is called scrapbooking for others, or S4O, and it's a wonderful way to get paid for doing something you love.

GETTING STARTED

It may feel daunting to turn a hobby into a business, but it can also be the perfect recipe for success. Mountaincow created Scrapbooking Pro for Windows as the first software specifically made for professional scrapbook printing for others. Scrapbooking Pro is very easy to use and works with any printer, scanner, and digital camera you already own; any printer-compatible paper, cardstock, or photo paper; plus all the rib-bons and embellishments you already own.

SAMPLE THIS

Your first step is to create a sample book or Web gallery portfolio to show your potential customers. If you plan to just have them browse through years and years of your scrapbooks, they'll be overwhelmed and have a hard time choosing one type of style. You'll be running around trying to find all the mate-rials that may no longer exist.

Instead, choose your favorite layouts that are easy to reproduce. Choose a variety of styles and subject matters so your customers can find something appropriate for anything from a wedding to a baby. You can also get started with the layouts provided in the Scrapbooking Pro software, customizing them as you like before printing and assembling them.

If you plan to create a website, you can make your sample book completely digital. Print the samples to graphics files and post them on your website or on scrapbook layout sharing websites such as twopeasinabucket.com.

COST OF DOING BUSINESS

Determining how much to charge others for your work can be difficult, but Scrapbooking Pro has a built-in print counter and clock to track time and materials used for each proj-ect. Start deciding upon an hourly or per-page rate to charge by thinking about how much money you need to pay for your materials and your time. The software is also designed to store project information such as materials used so you can keep track of how much the embellishments, paper, and glue cost to make the layout.

LAYOUT TO ORDER

Once your customer has chosen the style of scrapbook she wants and is ready to pass her photos to you, take careful notes about the sequence of the photos, who is in them, and the importance of them being included. Using digital photos will give you full reign to crop or alter them any way you like. If you are getting original photos, consider scan-ning them into your computer and working with a duplicate.

You can involve your customer during the process by first laying out the photos into a book and then emailing her each layout and asking her to email you some thoughts to incorporate into a journal for the page. Seeing the photos grouped, cropped, and designed into a layout with graphics, colors, and patterns will help cure any writer's block that may have prevented getting journal text at the initial meeting.

BUILD YOUR RESUME

A good way to start positioning yourself as a professional scrapbooker is to get published. Submit your layouts to magazines and enter contests as often as possible, using digital submissions to save time and money. Do a few jobs for friends and local businesses and make a second copy of each to put into your portfolio along with a referral quote about how great it was to work with you.

Talk to businesses in your area about hiring you to create pages for all their employees from the office holiday party photos, first day at work, or annual company picnic or offsite event. These can be nice, affordable ways for a company to appreciate its employees and can mean real dollars for you at a rate of $25 to $50 (£14 to £28) per page produced.

OTHER BUSINESS POSSIBILITIES

Scrapbooking for others is not the only way to make a profit from scrapbooking. Consider some other options:

- Buy and customize blank scrapbooks for babies or weddings for others to add their own photos. Market your books as the perfect shower gift and always include your contact information on your products.

- Use your scrapbook supplies to make greeting cards. Offer bulk rates at holiday time.

- Teach workshops at senior centers, YMCAs or JCCs, and local craft stores. Determine the skill level of each audience and adjust your material accordingly. Hands-on classes are always the most successful, so factor in the cost of your materials when calculating the admission rate you charge for the class.

- Find a position on a manufacturer's design team. Visit company websites to look for a call for designers. Larger companies refresh their team every year for new ideas, and some will work with freelance designers.

Project Details

COOLING OFF

Sample layouts such as "Cooling Off" were created by award-winning designers and included in Scrapbooking Pro software for you to use as a template. Swap your customer's photos for the ones used and change the text for easy, beautiful, customized layouts.

You may not be able to say the word "sprinkler", but you know how to stay cool on a hot summer day. Who knew a hose could be so fun?

Cooling Off

FINDING THE BEST MIX OF PAPER AND DIGITAL SCRAPBOOKING FOR YOU

So many of us love the idea of scrapbooking but are pressed for time. "Easy scrapbooking" means using your computer to assist you in whatever way possible to keep that box of un-scrapped photos or the folders of pictures on your computer at a minimum.

The first step is to choose your software. This book recommends the Mountaincow scrapbooking software for its ease of use, powerful design tools, and layered printing options. You can, however, apply the techniques discussed below to any software you choose to work with, including photo editors, paint programs, word processors, and so forth.

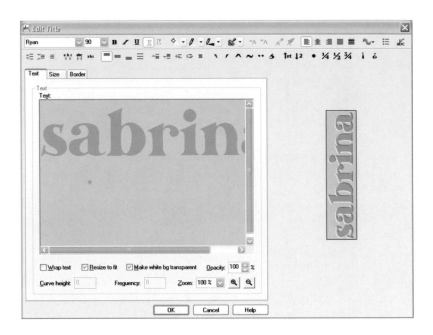

designing using the mountaincow scrapbooking software

WORKING WITH PAGES

You can easily create new pages from one of the built-in templates or from a new, blank page of any size. You can create a new scrapbook project that can have as many pages as you like in it, and the pages can be one or two-page spreads.

WORKING WITH TEXT

Using software specifically for scrapbooking or graphic design enables you to make creative titles and journals anywhere on your page. In addition to aligning text to the left, center or right, text can also be rotated, shaped vertically, or into waves, circles or spirals, and have any or all of the following effects applied to it:

- **Curved text** shapes the text along a bend, double-bend, wave, circle, spiral, semicircle, or quarter circle. The amplitude and frequency of the curve can be adjusted for bends, and multiple lines and styles of text will all follow the curve selected with circles being drawn concentric.

- **Background colored or patterned text** fills the area behind the text with a solid color or a pattern, bounded by the border (if any).

- **Bordered text** draws a solid-colored or patterned border around the text box in a variety of shapes, including rectangles, ovals, hearts, stars, tags, and more. The border can have separate inner and outer

lines in a contrasting color if desired.•
Colored text fills the letters with one or more different shades and colors. One nice effect is to highlight a single word from a paragraph using a contrasting color. You can also use a different color for each letter in a word.

- **Embossed text** displays with a shadowed edge giving it a three-dimensional rise above the background of the page.

- **Engraved text** displays with a shadowed edge giving it a three-dimensional depth into the background of the page.

- **Fully justified text** spaces the letters in each line so they line up at the left and right edges.

- **Horizontally spaced text** adjusts the spacing between letters for an entire line of text.

- **Kerned text** adjusts the spacing between individual letters to adjust for letter combinations that need more or less space.

- **Point-size justified text** scales each line to a larger or smaller point size so it lines up at the left and right edges.

- **Outlined text** borders the text with a second color, giving it an edge for two-tone or bubble lettering styles.

- **Patterned text** fills the letters in the text with one or more different colorful patterns. The patterns can be scaled to an appropriate size, given the point size of the text.

- **Random jitter text** randomizes the vertical location of each letter similar to a kidnappers ransom note.

- **Rotated text** lets you turn text on its side or on an angle to fit into a corner or along a vertical edge of a page.

- **Transparent text** lets you see the background, photo, or overlapping words through the text. You can adjust the setting to make the text more or less transparent or opaque.

- **Vertical text** rotates the letters so they read from top to bottom instead of left to right. Use the alignment to hang text from the top, bottom, center, or fully justified in the box.

- **Vertically justified text** adjusts the spacing between the lines of the text to evenly fill the box.

- **Vertically spaced text** adjusts the spacing between the lines of the text to fill more or less of the box. This can also be used to semi-overlap lines of text for overlapping transparent text.

WORKING WITH PHOTOS

Import your photos to Mountaincow's scrapbooking software and take advantage of the photo editing tools to enhance your photos. The software can import or paste in most standard graphics formats, including:

- **JPEG:** Joint Photographic Experts Group, pronounced "jay-peg," is the best format for photos but may cause distortions around solid graphical lines.

- **PNG:** Portable Network Graphics, pronounced "ping," is the best format for graphics.

- **GIF:** Graphics Interchange Format, pronounced "giff," is an older format for graphics limited to 256 colors.

- **TIFF:** Tagged Interchange File Format, pronounced "tiff," is a widely used format for sharing graphics of any type and ensuring no distortions occur in any kind of image.

- **EMF:** Enhanced Metafile Format, pronounced "metafile," is the best format for graphics that include line art or text and need to be printed at high resolutions.

- **BMP:** Bitmap, pronounced "bump," is the standard, uncompressed file format for Windows.

Many built-in photo editing features in the Mountaincow scrapbooking software make it easy to edit your photos without spending a ton of time learning expert photo editing software packages.

- **Blur** the image to have it fade into the background and layer text or other elements over it.

- **Brightness** adjusts the image to be brighter or darker.

- **Crop** to cut out a distracting background from any edge of the photo, or feature a specific area of the photo.

- **Duplicate** the images so you can have multiple copies on a page, possibly recolored, flipped, semi-overlapping, or rotated.

- **Faded-edge border** is an effect that blends the edges of the photo into the background in a variety of shapes including rectangles, ovals, hearts, stars, and more. The rate of diffusion can be adjusted.

- **Flip** the image horizontally or vertically to change the direction someone is facing or reposition a landscape to work better in your layout.

- **Frame inset** allows the frame to crop the image closer to or further from the edge of the image.

- **Grayscale images** are completely desaturated so there is no color at all and the lightness and darkness of the image is represented using only shades of gray from white to black.

- **Hue** adjusts the color tone of an image around the color wheel.

- **Make white transparent** in a graphic to avoid the white corners from showing up around a nonrectangular image when overlapping a background.

- **Patterned frame** allows any solid line frame to be filled with a chosen pattern instead of a solid color. The pattern can be scaled to match the width of the frame.

- **Recolor** the image to match an RGB value by simultaneously adjusting the hue, saturation, and brightness of the image.

- **Resize** the image so it fits the dimensions of your layout.

- **Rotate** the image to angle it to fit into your layout or to orient it along a vertical or diagonal edge.

- **Tint** the image to match an RGB value by first converting it to grayscale and then simultaneously adjusting the hue, saturation, and brightness of the image. For example, you can create a sepia effect when tinted an image to a dark yellow.

- **Transparency** adjusts the amount by which the background shows through an image, and in the process also lightens the image.

- **Saturation** adjusts the intensity of the color in an image, with zero percent saturation creating a grayscale image.

- **Solid-line frame** allows any image to be clipped into a shaped frame in a variety of shapes including rectangles, ovals, hearts, stars, tags, and more. The frame can have a solid color as well as a different color outline and inner line in varying thicknesses.

Add one of three types of borders for your images: A decorative design such as a polka-dot border; a custom shape such as an oval, heart, or diamond in any color or width; or fade the edges of the image to have it blend into the page.

Match the elements on your page, such as your text or borders, to your photos by using the color sample tool. As you move your cursor over your photo, the color below will be previewed in the Sample Color window and can be applied to whatever is selected.

WORKING WITH PATTERNS

Fill your text, shapes, backgrounds, and borders with patterns. Select a designed pattern or create your own using the pattern creator. The pattern creator lets you quickly and easily create a repeatable pattern such as polka dots, stripes, and more. Start by choosing a shape and an alternate shape, then adjust the spacing between the shapes, give each shape its own color and outline, stagger the rows, or even substitute your own graphics for the shapes. Customize further by adjusting the scale, color, or rotation of the pattern.

CREATING SHAPES AND FRAMES

Add shapes to your layout as a decorative detail or as a mat for your photo. Choose from shapes such as lips, tags, stars, and more. Fill with patterns or colors and outline with borders. You can print a photo or text box with a frame around it so it is already matted and ready to place on your layout. You can also print out frames by themselves and cut out the middles to place as mats over photograph prints you already have.

printing the entire layout

CHOOSE A LAYOUT SIZE

Printing your entire layout at once means your pages will be flat. It also means you will need to choose paper and a printer that will fit your desired layout size (the most common include 12" x 12" [30.9 x 30.9 cm], 8.5" x 11" [21.6 x 27.9 cm], 8" x 10" [20.3 x 25.4 cm], 8" x 8" [20.3 x 20.3 cm], and 6" x 6" [15.2 x 15.2 cm]). For this reason, many scrapbookers who print the entire page choose to work with the standard 8.5" x 11" (21.6 x 27.9 cm) printers and photo paper they already own. Several companies, such as Epson, have introduced wide-format printers and 13" x 18" (33 x 45.7 cm) glossy photo paper to print 12" x 12" (30.9 x 30.9 cm) full-bleed layouts at home.

Sometimes the size you choose for your layout depends on the book you intend to insert the pages into. Many companies are producing cute books in smaller sizes than the traditional 12" x 12" (30.9 x 30.9 cm) size, so if someone gives you a 6" x 6" (15.2 x 15.2 cm) brag book, have fun seeing how different your layouts turn out when working with such a small page.

When thinking about choosing a layout size, you may also want to consider what you intend to use your layouts for. If you want to enter the layout into contests or submit it to magazines for publication, the standard page size is 12" x 12" (30.9 x 30.9 cm), so check the rules for submissions before using a different size. If you want to upload the pages to a photo sharing website, such as Kodak Gallery, for photo or calendar printing, the largest economical size to use is typically 8" x 10" (20.3 x 25.4 cm).

CHOOSE YOUR PAPER

You may want to consider only using archival-safe paper for your scrapbooks to ensure their longevity. All craft and scrapbook stores and websites will indicate papers that are acid and lignin free.

You'll also want to make sure the paper you chose will easily go though your printer. If using cardstock—a thicker paper measured in pounds—you'll generally want to stay under 80 pound, or 218 g/sm cover stock. When in doubt, it's always best to purchase in small quantities so you can do a test print first. Also, whenever possible, buy the photo paper branded for the printer you have (e.g. Epson paper for Epson printers) since the papers are formulated to work best with their ink.

CHOOSE YOUR PRINTER

The two main types of printers available today are ink-jet and laser. Modern ink-jet printers transfer tiny droplets of ink onto paper to create full-color images. The ink dries very quickly and typically will not smudge unless it gets wet. Photo-quality ink-jet printers use six ink colors instead of four to better blend skin tones.

Laser printers roll toner onto the surface of the paper and bind it to the paper with a hot roller called a fuser. They can achieve very fine print strokes for script typefaces and can print on paper that is not absorbent, including metallic and vellum, but the toner may not fuse well to roughly textured papers. Also, solid blocks of color will be halftoned, which means they will print in small dots similar to the way a magazine looks when viewed very closely.

keeping it digital

PRINTING TO A GRAPHICS FILE

You can also keep your layout entirely in the digital realm and never actually print, cut, or paste again if you like. You can post your layouts to your own website or a layout sharing website such as twopeasinabucket.com. You can email your layout to family and friends or post it to a photo sharing website and let them order prints. You can even create a high-resolution graphics file to be sent to a professional print shop for use in printing brochures or even super large prints to frame and hang on the wall.

Because layouts typically have photos, JPEG will usually be the best graphics file format to save your layout using the Print to Graphics file feature in Mountaincow's scrapbooking software. However, if you are sending the file to a printer, choose TIFF (compressed) at 300 or 600 dpi to ensure you have enough detail around the text in your journals and the lines in your graphics.

PUBLISHING TO A WEBSITE

Most photo-sharing websites require images to be JPEG format to upload a file. Determine the requirements of the website before you print your layouts to digital files. The online community has expanded astoundingly for scrapbookers looking to share their layouts and get tips on materials and design ideas. Try posting your favorite layouts and see how many people comment on your ideas and "borrow" your suggestions for layouts of their own. Before you know it, people from around the country may be emailing you asking when you will be posting a new design!

SUBMITTING YOUR LAYOUTS TO MAGAZINES

Magazines often prefer layouts to be submitted via email rather than being sent a hard copy. This can save you a ton of time, money, and effort since you do not need to produce an extra copy every time you want to submit a layout to a different magazine. You also don't have to wait for an answer from one magazine at a time. Another benefit to you, aside from saving a trip to the post office, is you don't have to worry about not having your layout returned. Find out the format the magazine requires before printing your layouts to a digital file.

When emailing a layout, choose screen resolution so the file is as small as possible for easy emailing. When it comes time for publication, the magazine will ask you for a high-resolution, or "high-res" file they can print with sufficient detail. This should be at least 300 or 600 dpi and will result in a large file size, so you will need to burn it to a CD to mail it to the editor.

walking the line between paper and digital

CREATING THE LAYOUT ON SCREEN

Your scrapbooking MO may evolve a bit as you become more comfortable using the computer for various bits and pieces of the process. One valuable use of the computer is to create a template or try out your layout before actually putting scissors to paper.

Start from one of the built-in layout templates or just from a blank page or spread. Use the page view to create your layout by adding images, titles, journals, shapes, and frames and dragging them to position them where you like. This way you can size your photos, create your title, and write your journal all to fit, and you can see what looks good with these particular photos and text.

CHOOSING OR PRINTING A BACKGROUND

Often you will be using a 12" x 12" (30.9 x 30.9 cm) piece of scrapbook paper you've purchased from a craft store for your page background, but you can also custom print a background color or pattern onto your own paper. If you've designed a background to print, select the Shapes and Frames icon on the left of your screen. Select the background and choose Print.

PRINTING ELEMENTS ONTO 8.5" X 11" (21.6 X 27.9 CM) SHEETS

Mountaincow's scrapbooking software makes it easy to print elements from your layout template individually with crop marks for easy trimming. To print, for example, all your photos on photo paper, choose the Image icon on the left of your screen to view all the images and choose Print. You can do the same for all your titles, journals, shapes, and frames.

By choosing Print, all the photos on this layout will be tiled onto 8.5" x 11" (21.6 x 27.9 cm) pages with crop marks so you can trim and add them to your background page. This is a great way to conserve photo paper since the program automatically arranges the photos efficiently onto the size sheet you are printing. View the page again to refer back to your layout template to position and adhere photos, titles, and journals in the right place.

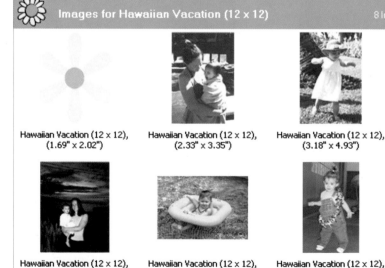

CUTTING AND PASTING

There is a wide variety of scissors, paper trimmers, and punches available for all different purposes. Choose according to what you create most.

Craft scissors: sharp scissors for cutting around letters and hard to reach places.

Craft knife: sharp blade for creating openings on flat surfaces.

Decorative-edge scissors: scissors with a scalloped or zigzag blade for creating decorative edges.

Paper trimmer: desktop tool for cutting straight edges.

Large punches: for multiples of even squares or circles.

 See the Bonus CD for Five Must-have Tools how-to video.

Glue, tape, and paste also come in a variety of types. You may want to consider choosing an acid-free adhesive to ensure the longevity of your scrapbook. Choose your glue or tape by what you plan to adhere. If you tend to use heavy embellishments, such as hinges or metal tags, you will need something far tackier than if you use paper die-cuts. Read the adhesive packaging to determine its best use. See page 90 for more information about adhesives.

EMBELLISHING

Embellishments can add dimension and design to scrapbook pages. Once you have printed and assembled your page, you can adhere any store-bought embellishments. You can also customize embellishments by printing on store-bought labels or tags using the Stickers view in the Mountaincow scrapbooking software. You can add images, text, colors, and patterns to the stickers to create embellishments that completely coordinate with the other printed elements on your pages.

index

about the author

Patty Hoffman Brahe has always been a "saver"—of ticket stubs, photographs, and just about every letter she's ever received. Her earliest albums are mostly limited to camp photos and her friends' names drawn in bubble letters, but once her older brother passed along a hand-me-down computer, Patty's world—and her scrapbooks—changed forever. Her love of using a computer to make creative titles and journals for her albums, plus making her own party invitations, took a professional turn years later when she joined Mountaincow, the creators of invitation and scrapbooking software, as director of communications. Patty is also the author of *Easy Invitations* (Quarry Books, 2005). She lives with her husband in New York City where she runs a stationery consulting business, P's of Paper.